"BE·MUCH OCCUPIED WITH JESUS"

SEA HARP PRESS

LETTERS from SPIRITUAL GUIDES

SPURGEON
TOZER • EDWARDS
MURRAY • LUTHER
À KEMPIS • and more

Compiled by Eugene Luning

Authors: Charles H. Spurgeon, Eusebius, Meister Eckhart, Jonathan Edwards, William Beveridge, J.C. Ryle, Irenaeus, Abraham Kuyper, S.D. Gordon, George Griffin, William Law, Hannah Whitall Smith, Paul Wernle, Basil the Great, J.B. Phillips, George Herbert, Andrew Murray, Henry Drummond, Edmund de Pressensé, Martin Luther, Gerhard Tersteegen, Origen, Hippolytus of Rome, Søren Kierkegaard, Thérèse of Lisieux, Daniel Steele, A.W. Tozer, François Fénelon, Charles Finney, John Owen, Albert the Great, Frances Havergal, Thomas à Kempis, John Flavel, Joseph Addison, William Penn, Anselm, John Henry Jowett, Jean-Pierre de Caussade, D.L. Moody

This book and all other Sea Harp books are available at Christian bookstores and distributors worldwide.

For more information on foreign distributors, call 717-532-3040.

Reach us on the Internet: www.seaharp.com

ISBN 13 TP: 978-0-7684-6477-1

ISBN 13 eBook: 978-0-7684-6478-8

For Worldwide Distribution

1 2 3 4 5 6 7 8 / 27 26 25 24 23

CONTENTS

To Be Visited by Him in Love

Charles H. Spurgeon

We are writing to you about something which has always existed yet which we ourselves actually saw and heard: something which we had an opportunity to observe closely and even to hold in our hands, and yet, as we know now, was something of the very Word of life himself! For it was life which appeared before us: we saw it, we are eye-witnesses of it, and are now writing to you about it. It was the very life of all ages, the life that has always existed with the Father, which actually became visible in person to us mortal men. We repeat, we really saw and heard what we are now writing to you about. We want you to be with us in this—in this fellowship with the Father, and Jesus Christ his Son. We must write and tell you about it, because the more that fellowship extends the greater the joy it brings to us who are already in it.

(1 John 1:1-4, Phillips)

Dear Downcast Soul,

It is a theme for wonder that the glorious God should visit sinful man. "What is man, that Thou art mindful of him? and the son of man, that Thou visitest him?" A divine visit is a joy to be treasured whenever we are favoured with it. David speaks of it with great solemnity. The Psalmist was not content barely to speak of it; but he wrote it down in plain terms, that it might be known throughout all generations: "Thou hast visited me in the night." Beloved, if God has ever visited you, you also will marvel at it, will carry it in your memory, will speak of it to your friends, and will record it in your diary as one of the notable events of your life. Above all, you will speak of it to God Himself, and say with adoring gratitude, "Thou hast visited me in the night." It should be a solemn part of worship to remember and make known the condescension of the Lord, and say, both in lowly prayer and in joyful psalm, "Thou hast visited me."...

For our Lord to visit us is something more than for us to have the assurance of our salvation, though that is very delightful, and none of us should rest satisfied unless we possess it. To know that Jesus loves me, is one thing; but to be visited by Him in love, is more.

Nor is it simply a close contemplation of Christ; for we can picture Him as exceedingly fair and majestic, and yet not have Him consciously near us. Delightful and instructive as it is to behold the likeness of Christ by meditation, yet the enjoyment of His actual presence is something more. I may wear my friend's portrait about my person, and yet may not be able to say, "Thou hast visited me."...

At such a time there is a delightful sense of rest; we have no ambitions, no desires. A divine serenity and security envelop us. We have no thought of foes, or fears, or afflictions, or doubts. There is a joyous laying aside of our own will. We are nothing, and we will nothing: Christ is everything, and His will is the pulse of our soul. We are perfectly content either to be ill or to be well, to be rich or to be poor, to be slandered or to be honoured, so that we may but abide in the love of Christ. Jesus fills the horizon of our being.

At such a time a flood of great joy will fill our minds. We shall half wish that the morning may never break again, for fear its light should banish the superior light of Christ's presence. We shall wish that we could glide away with our Beloved to the place where He feedeth among the lilies. We long to hear the voices of the white-robed armies, that we may follow their glorious Leader whithersoever He goeth. I am persuaded that there is no great actual distance between earth and heaven: the distance lies in our dull minds. When the Beloved visits us in the night, He makes our chambers to be the vestibule of His palace-halls. Earth rises to heaven when heaven comes down to earth....

Have your hearts right with Him, and He will visit you often, until every day you shall walk with God, as Enoch did, and so turn week-days into Sabbaths, meals into sacraments, homes into temples, and earth into heaven. So be it with us!

Your friend and His,

CHARLES SPURGEON

Questions for consideration:

1. When was the hour or season in which Jesus felt closest to you?

2. How would you describe His proximity now, today?

The Coming of the Messenger of the Great Counsel

Eusebius

At the beginning God expressed himself. That personal expression, that word, was with God, and was God, and he existed with God from the beginning. All creation took place through him, and none took place without him. In him appeared life and this life was the light of mankind. The light still shines in the darkness and the darkness has never put it out... This was the true light which shines upon every man as he comes into the world. He came into the world—the world he had created—and the world failed to recognise him. He came into his own creation, and his own people would not accept him. Yet wherever men did accept him he gave them the power to become sons of God.

(John 1:1-5, 9-12, Phillips)

Dear Seeker,

No language is sufficient to express the origin and the worth, the being and the nature of Christ. Wherefore also the divine Spirit says in the prophecies, "Who shall declare his generation?" For none knoweth the Father except the Son, neither can any one know the Son adequately except the Father alone who hath begotten him.

For who beside the Father could clearly understand the Light which was before the world, the intellectual and essential Wisdom which existed before the ages, the living Word which was in the beginning with the Father and which was God, the first and only begotten of God which was before every creature and creation visible and invisible, the commander-in-chief of the rational and immortal host of heaven, the messenger of the great counsel, the executor of the Father's unspoken will, the creator, with the Father, of all things, the second cause of the universe after the Father, the true and only-begotten Son of God, the Lord and God and King of all created things, the one who has received dominion and power, with divinity itself, and with might and honor from the Father; as it is said in regard to him in the mystical passages of Scripture which speak of his divinity: "In the beginning was the Word, and the Word was with God, and the

Word was God." "All things were made by him; and without him was not anything made."

Do you know that you know *that* One?

Your friend and His,

ΕΥΣΕΒΙΟΥ

EUSEBIUS

Questions for consideration:

1. What worship song or hymn is grabbing your heart most these days? Any particular lines or stanzas that are standing out?

2. What is your favorite title for Jesus? (*ie.* God With Us, Savior, Lord, King of Kings, etc.) Why?

LETTER 3

God Yearning after Us

Meister Eckhart

Consider the incredible love that the Father has shown us in allowing us to be called "children of God"—and that is not just what we are called, but what we are. Our heredity on the Godward side is no mere figure of speech—which explains why the world will no more recognise us than it recognised Christ. Oh, dear children of mine (forgive the affection of an old man!), have you realised it? Here and now we are God's children. We don't know what we shall become in the future. We only know that, if reality were to break through, we should reflect his likeness, for we should see him as he really is! Everyone who has at heart a hope like that keeps himself pure, for he knows how pure Christ is.

(1 John 3:1-3, Phillips)

Beloved,

Our Lord Jesus Christ hath in the Gospel spoken with His own blessed lips these words, which signify, "No man can come to Me unless My Father draw him." In another place He says, "I am in the Father and the Father in Me." Therefore whoever cometh to the Son cometh to the Father. Further, He saith, "I and the Father are One. Therefore whomsoever the Father draweth, the Son draweth likewise." St Augustine also saith, "The works of the Holy Trinity are inseparable from each other." Therefore the Father draweth to the Son, and the Son draweth to the Holy Ghost, and the Holy Ghost draweth to the Father and the Son; and each Person of the Trinity, when He draweth to the Two Others, draweth to Himself, because the Three are One. The Father draweth with the might of His power, the Son draweth with His unfathomable wisdom, the Holy Ghost draweth with His love. Thus we are drawn by the Sacred Trinity with the cords of Power, Wisdom and Love, when we are drawn from an evil thing to a good thing, and from a good thing to a better, and from a better thing to the best of all....

Therefore the Son came down from heaven, and was incarnate of a Virgin, and took upon Him all our bodily weaknesses, except sin and folly, into which Adam had cast us; and out of all His words and works and limbs and nerves, He made a cord, and drew us so skillfully, and so heartily, that the bloody sweat poured from His sacred Body. And when He had drawn men without ceasing for three and thirty years, He saw the beginnings of a movement and the redemption of all things that would follow. Therefore He said, "And I, if I be lifted up on the Cross, will draw all men unto Me."...

All that God worketh and teacheth, He worketh in His Son. All His work is directed to this end that we also may be His Son. When God sees that we are indeed His Son, He yearns after us, and in the depth of His Divine Being waves of longing break forth, to reveal to us the abyss of His Godhead, and the fullness of His essence; He hastens to identify Himself with us. Herein He hath joy and gladness in full measure.

Remember all this.

Meister Eckhart

MEISTER ECKHART

Questions for consideration:

1. Do you have a "favorite moment" from the life of Jesus in the four Gospels?

2. When you think of His attributes, which of the Old Testament prophecies of His coming come to mind for you?

The Light of the Wisdom of God

Jonathan Edwards

The spirit of this world has blinded the minds of those who do not believe, and prevents the light of the glorious Gospel of Christ, the image of God, from shining on them. For it is Christ Jesus the Lord whom we preach, not ourselves; we are your servants for his sake. God, who first ordered 'light to shine in darkness', has flooded our hearts with his light. We now can enlighten men only because we can give them knowledge of the glory of God, as we see it in the face of Jesus Christ.

(2 Corinthians 4:4-6, Phillips)

My Dear Friend,

Jesus is the most excellent and divine wisdom that any creature is capable of. He is more excellent than any human learning; He is far more excellent than all the knowledge of the greatest philosophers or statesmen. Yea, the least glimpse of the glory of God in the face of Christ doth more exalt and ennoble the soul, than all the knowledge of those that have the greatest speculative understanding in divinity without grace. This knowledge has the most noble object that is or can be, *viz.*, the divine glory or excellency of God and Christ. The knowledge of these objects is that wherein consists the most excellent knowledge of the angels, yea, of God himself.

This knowledge is that which is above all others sweet and joyful. Men have a great deal of pleasure in human knowledge, in studies of natural things; but this is nothing to that joy which arises from this divine light shining into the soul. This light gives a view of those things that are immensely the most exquisitely beautiful, and capable of delighting the eye of the understanding. This spiritual light is the dawning of the light of glory in the heart. There is nothing so powerful as this to support persons in affliction, and to give the mind peace and brightness in this stormy and dark world.

This light is such as effectually influences the inclination, and changes the nature of the soul. It assimilates the nature to the divine nature, and changes the soul into an image of the same glory that is beheld. 2 Corinthians 3:18 **says**, "But we all with open face, beholding as in a glass the glory of the Lord, are changed into the same image, from glory to glory, even as by the Spirit of the Lord." This knowledge will wean from the world, and raise the inclination to heavenly things. It will turn the heart to God as the fountain of good, and to choose him for the only portion. This light, and this only, will bring the soul to a saving close with Christ. It conforms the heart to the gospel, mortifies its enmity and opposition against the scheme of salvation therein revealed: it causes the heart to embrace the joyful tidings, and entirely to adhere to, and acquiesce in the revelation of Christ as our Saviour: it causes the whole soul to accord and symphonize with it, admitting it with entire credit and respect cleaving to it with full inclination and affection; and it effectually disposes the soul to give up itself entirely to Christ.

This light, and this only, has its fruit in a universal holiness of life. No merely notional or speculative understanding of the doctrines of religion will ever bring to this. But this light, as it reaches the bottom of the heart, and changes the nature, so it will effectually dispose to a universal obedience. It shows God's worthiness to be obeyed and served. It draws forth the heart in a sincere love to God, which is the only principle of a true, gracious, and universal obedience; and it convinces of the reality of those glorious rewards that God has promised to them that obey him.

Your friend and His,

Jonathan Edwards

JONATHAN EDWARDS

Questions for consideration:

1. What does it mean to you that Jesus is the "light of the world"?

2. What does it currently mean that Jesus is the "light" in your own life?

LETTER 5

Tasting and Seeing His Goodness

William Beveridge

I look upon everything as loss compared with the over-whelming gain of knowing Jesus Christ my Lord. For his sake I did in actual fact suffer the loss of everything, but I considered it useless rubbish compared with being able to win Christ. For now my place is in him, and I am not dependent upon any of the self-achieved righteousness of the Law. God has given me that genuine righteousness which comes from faith in Christ. How changed are my ambitions!

(Philippians 3:8,9, Phillips)

Dear Hungry Heart,

We must not think that it is enough to know in general that there is a God, and that he is wise and powerful, great and glorious, true and faithful, good and gracious; these things a man may know in general, so as to be able to discourse of them, and dispute for them too, and yet come short of that knowledge which is requisite to our true serving of God: which should be such a knowledge as will not only swim in the brain, but sink down into the heart; whereby a man is possessed with a due sense of those things he knows, so that he doth not only know, but in a manner feel them to he so. Thus David, who, in **that** text, calls upon his son to "know the God of his fathers," intimates elsewhere what knowledge he means: saying, "Oh taste and see that the Lord is good." Where we may observe, how he requires our spiritual senses to be employed in our knowledge of God, so as to see that he is good, yea, and taste it too; that is, feel and experience it in ourselves; ...if we be but careful and constant in our meditations upon God, and sincere in performing our devotions to him, for by these means our notions of God will be refined, our conceptions cleared, and our affections, by consequence, so moved towards him, **then** we shall taste and experience in ourselves, as well as know from others, that he is good, and that all perfections are concentered in him.

But this practical and experimental knowledge of God doth necessarily presuppose the other, or the general knowledge of him, so as to be acquainted with the several expressions which God in Scripture hath made use of, whereby to reveal himself and his perfections to us; as when he is pleased to call himself the almighty God, the all-wise and infinite, the just and gracious God, and the like; or to say of himself, "I am that I am"; that is, in and of myself eternal. Unless we first know that these and such like expressions belong to God, and what is the true meaning and purport of them, it is impossible for us to arrive at that knowledge of him, which is necessary to our serving him aright.

And I come to the last thing to be considered here concerning the knowledge of God, even that it is necessary to our serving him; so that none can serve him that does not first know him, and therefore that the method, as well as matter of David's advice is here observable: "Know thou the God of thy fathers, and serve him"; or, first know him, and then serve him "with a perfect heart and a willing mind."

And verily one would think that this is a truth so clear, so evident of itself, that it needs no proof or demonstration; for how is it possible for us to know how to serve God, unless we first know that God whom we ought to serve? for all our services unto God should be both proper to his nature, and suitable to his perfections; and therefore, unless I first know his nature and perfections, how can I adjust my services to them? As, for example, I am to fear his greatness, and trust on his mercy, and rejoice in his goodness, and desire his favour: but how can I do this, unless I know that he is thus great and merciful, good and favourable?

Consider those questions for yourself.

WILLIAM BEVERIDGE

WILLIAM BEVERIDGE

Questions for consideration:

1. What is your current pattern for your personal devotions?

2. Do those times feel rich and exciting? Or dry and a bit dull? Why do you answer that way?

The Rest within Reach

J.C. Ryle

There still exists, therefore, a full and complete rest for the people of God. And he who experiences his real rest is resting from his own work as fully as God from his. Let us then be eager to know this rest for ourselves, and let us beware that no one misses it through falling into the same kind of unbelief as those we have mentioned. For the Word that God speaks is alive and active; it cuts more keenly than any two-edged sword: it strikes through to the place where soul and spirit meet, to the innermost intimacies of a man's being: it exposes the very thoughts and motives of a man's heart. No creature has any cover from the sight of God; everything lies naked and exposed before the eyes of him with whom we have to do.

(Hebrews 4:9-13, Phillips)

Dear Weary Wanderer,

Look, to begin with, at the great mysterious truth which lies at the foundation of our holy faith, the incarnation of Christ. When the Eternal Son of God came down into this sin-burdened world, to bring redemption, and change the whole condition of our fallen race, how did He come? Not as a mighty angel or a glorious spirit, as we might have expected. Nothing of the kind! He took on Him a bodily nature, just like our own, sin only excepted. He was born of a woman as an infant, and had a body that grew and increased in stature as our bodies do,—a body that could hunger and thirst, and be weary and need sleep, and feel pain, and groan in agony and suffering, like the body of any one who reads **from** this paper. In that body He condescended to tabernacle for thirty-three years, its members daily fulfilling the Law of God perfectly, so that in His "flesh" Satan could find nothing failing or defective (John 14:30)....

Now, rest for the labouring and heavy-laden is one of the chief promises which the Word of God offers to man, both in the Old Testament and the New. "Come to me," says the world, "and I will give you riches and pleasure." "Come with me," says the devil, "and I will give you greatness, power, and wisdom." " Come unto Me," says the Lord Jesus Christ, "and I will give you rest." "Walk in the old paths," says the prophet Jeremiah, "and you shall find rest for your souls."

But what is the nature of that rest which the Lord Jesus promises to give? It is no mere repose of body. A man may have that, and yet be miserable. You may place him in a palace, and surround him with every possible comfort; you may give him money in abundance, and everything that money can buy; you may free him from all care about to-morrow's bodily wants, and take away the need of labouring for a single hour: all this you may do to a man, and yet not give him true rest. Thousands know this only too well by bitter experience. Their hearts are starving in the midst of worldly plenty; their inward man is sick and weary, while their outward man is clothed in purple and fine linen, and fares sumptuously every day! Yes: a man may have houses, and lands, and money, and horses, and carriages, and soft beds, and good fare, and attentive servants and yet not have true "rest."...

True rest is the privilege of all believers in Christ. Some know more of it, and some less; some feel it only at distant intervals, and some feel it almost always. Few enjoy the sense of it without many a battle with unbelief, and many a conflict with fear: but all who truly come to Christ know something of this rest. Ask them, with all their complaints and doubts, whether they would give up Christ and go back to the world. You will get only one answer. Weak as their sense of rest may be, they have got hold of something which does them good, and that something they cannot let go.

Rest such as this is within reach of all who are willing to seek it and receive it. The poor man is not so poor but he may have it; the ignorant man is not so ignorant but he may know it; the sick man is not so weak and helpless but he may get hold of it. Faith, simple faith, is the one thing needful in order to possess Christ's rest. Faith in Christ is the grand secret of happiness. Neither poverty, nor ignorance, nor tribulation, nor distress can prevent men and women feeling rest of soul, if they will only come to Christ and believe.

Will you come to Christ and believe?

J. C. Liverpool

J.C. RYLE
BISHOP OF LIVERPOOL

Questions for consideration:

1. Do you equate "rest" with your life in Christ? Why or why not?

2. Write a description of how you picture Jesus. Consider His eyes, His face, the way He carries Himself. What would it be like to run into Him on the street?

"With You God"

Irenaeus

Blessings on the Lord, the God of Israel, because he has turned his face towards his people and has set them free! And he has raised up for us a standard of salvation in his servant David's house! Long, long ago, through the words of his holy prophets, he promised to do this for us, so that we should be safe from our enemies and secure from all who hate us. So does he continue the mercy he showed to our forefathers. So does he remember the holy agreement he made with them and the oath which he swore to our father Abraham, to make us this gift: that we should be saved from the hands of our enemies, and in his presence should serve him unafraid in holiness and righteousness all our lives.

(Luke 1:68-75, Phillips)

Dear Friend of God,

God the Father was very merciful: He sent His creative Word, who in coming to deliver us came to the very place and spot in which we had lost life, and broke the bonds of our fetters. And His light appeared and made the darkness of the prison disappear, and hallowed our birth and destroyed death, loosing those same fetters in which we were enchained....

Thus then the Word of God *in all things hath the pre-eminence*; for that He is true man and *Wonderful Counselor and Mighty God*; calling men anew to fellowship with God, that by fellowship with Him we may partake of incorruption. So then He who was proclaimed by the law through Moses, and by the prophets of the Most High and Almighty God, as Son of the Father of all; He from whom all things are, He who spake with Moses—He came into Judea, generated from God by the Holy Spirit, and born of the Virgin Mary, even of her who was of the seed of David and of Abraham, Jesus the Anointed of God, showing Himself to be the One who was proclaimed beforehand by the prophets....

Now Emmanuel is, being interpreted, *With you God*; or as a yearning cry uttered by the prophet, such as this: *With us shall be God*; according to which it is the explanation and manifestation of the good tidings proclaimed. For *Behold*, He saith, *the virgin shall conceive and shall bring forth a son*; and He, being God, is to be with us. And, as if altogether astonished at these things, he proclaims in regard to these future events that *With us shall be God....*

Therefore by newness of the spirit is our calling, and not in the oldness of the letter; even as Jeremiah prophesied: *Behold the days come, saith the Lord, that I will accomplish for the house of Israel and for the house of Judah the covenant: of the testament which I covenanted with their fathers, in the day when I took them by the hand to lead them out of the land of Egypt: because they continued not in the covenant, and I regarded them not, saith the Lord. For this is the covenant of the testament that I will covenant with the house of Israel after those days, saith the Lord: I will put my laws into their minds, and write them in their hearts; and I will be to them a God, and they shall be to me a people: and they shall not teach any more every man his neighbour, and every man his brother, saying, Know the Lord: for all shall know me, from the least to the greatest of them. For I will pardon and be merciful unto the sins of their iniquities, and their sins will I remember no more....*

This, beloved, is the preaching of the truth, and this is the manner of our redemption, and this is the way of life, which the prophets proclaimed, and Christ established....

Your friend and His,

ЄΙΡΗΝΑΪ

IRENAEUS

Questions for consideration:

1. How truly free in Jesus do you feel?

2. Better put: Are you the freest person you've ever met? Why or why not?

LETTER 8

Divine Life Near to the Heart

Abraham Kuyper

So the word of God became a human being and lived among us. We saw his splendour (the splendour as of a father's only son), full of grace and truth. And it was about him that John stood up and testified, exclaiming: "Here is the one I was speaking about when I said that although he would come after me he would always be in front of me; for he existed before I was born!" Indeed, every one of us has shared in his riches—there is a grace in our lives because of his grace. For while the Law was given by Moses, love and truth came through Jesus Christ. It is true that no one has ever seen God at any time. Yet the divine and only Son, who lives in the closest intimacy with the Father, has made him known.

(John 1:14-18, Phillips)

Dear Traveler,

When in foreign parts we unexpectedly hear our own language spoken we feel at home at once. This is because we feel that this language is common property between us and our fellow country-men. In it we live. By it they come closer to us than others who only speak a foreign tongue. This is still more strongly felt with regard to animals. Highly organized animals come very close to man. There often is a remarkable understanding between a shepherd or hunter and his dog, or between a rider and his horse. But close as this approach may be, an altogether different and far richer world opens itself to us when we meet a fellow man. He is flesh of our flesh, bone of our bone, with a soul like our own. And this creates fellowship which is far more intimate and tender, especially when the people we meet are of like tastes and aims of life with ours. There are classes, social distinctions and other divisions in the world of man. And if anyone would become more closely acquainted with us and invite mutual confidence, he should be one of our class and be embarked, as it were, on the sea of life in the same boat with us. And this is the meaning of Immanuel.

In the Babe of Bethlehem, God draws near to us in our nature, in order presently in our language, through the medium of our world of thought and with the aid of our representations, to make his presence felt in the heart, in accordance with the perceptions of which it is capable. He draws near to us in our nature, so that in order to find God we do not need to go out from our nature and enter upon a purely spiritual existence. Desirous to bless us, God from his side makes the transition which he spares us. We do not go to him, but he comes to us. We need not raise ourselves up to him, but he comes down to us that afterwards he may draw us up to himself. He enters into our nature. He assumes it and cradles in the Bethlehem manger with an existence which human nature brings with it. Here the distance between God and us is removed. The tension and effort to understand it purely spiritually is spared us. What we perceive is human nature. What presently we hear is human speech. What we observe are utterances of human life. An unknown brightness plays and glistens through it all and behind it all, a mysterious higher something, a something altogether holy. But now it does not repel, but it attracts and charms because it approaches us in our own human nature. The human nature of Immanuel is not merely a screen to temper dazzling glories, but the means and instrument to bring Divine Life unaffectedly and intimately near to the heart. It is as though human nature in us unites itself with human nature in Jesus in order to bring God into immediate contact with the soul.

We do not say that this was necessary by itself. The fact of our creation after the Divine Image seemed to give us every requisite for fellowship with God. But we must ever remember that sin ruined this Image. In this weakened and ruined estate nothing short of holy grace could fill the gap. This was done in Immanuel, in the coming of God to us in the garb of human nature. Idolatry proclaimed the need of this when it imaged the Lord of heaven and earth after the likeness of a man. Hence Christianity alone can undo idolatry and paganism, since in Immanuel it presents the true Image of God anew. The result itself has sealed this. In Christ alone pure fellowship with the living God has been realized and gloriously celebrated in Psalm and hymnody. Apart from Immanuel we have philosophy about God, denial of God, or at most idolatry and cold deism. In and through Immanuel alone there is life in God and with God, full of warmth, elevation and inspiration. In Immanuel God draws near to us in our own nature and through Immanuel the soul mounts from this nature spiritually up to the Father of spirits.

In Immanuel we have the way, but not the goal. It begins with Jesus, but in the end the Father himself makes tabernacle with us and the day breaks of which Jesus said: "In that day I say not unto you that I will pray the Father for you, for the Father himself loveth you." Then also the abundant activity of the Holy Ghost will unfold itself, even of the Comforter who could not come until after Jesus had been glorified. Let there not be anything artificial therefore or conventional in our seeking after God. No wilful, premeditated going out after Jesus to have fellowship with God. Immanuel brings us reconciliation, so that we dare to draw near again. He brings the Divine in human nature so that we can draw near again. We owe him the Word, the world of thoughts and representations, the blessed results of his work that are showered down upon us, and the supply of powers of the Kingdom which inwardly renew us. But underneath it all, personal contact, real fellowship with God, is always a hidden, spiritual motion, so that inwardly we hear his voice and we can say with Job: "Now mine eye seeth thee." This is fellowship with God as man with man. As with Jacob at Peniel.

Your friend and His,

ABRAHAM KUYPER

Questions for consideration:

1. What portion of the Christmas narrative most moves your heart and mind?

2. What is the most recent portion of Scripture that has "spoken" to you?

The Old Eden Language of Love

S.D. Gordon

It was right and proper that in bringing many sons to glory, God (from whom and by whom everything exists) should make the leader of their salvation a perfect leader through the fact that he suffered. For the one who makes men holy and the men who are made holy share a common humanity. So that he is not ashamed to call them his brothers, for he says: "I will declare your name to my brethren; in the midst of the congregation I will sing praise to you."

(Hebrews 2:10-12, Phillips)

Dear Child,

Jesus is God spelling Himself out in language that man can understand. God and man used to talk together freely. But one day man went away from God. And then he went farther away. He left home. He left his native land, Eden, where he lived with God. He emigrated from God. And through going away he lost his mother-tongue.

A language always changes away from its native land. Through going away from his native land man lost his native speech. Through not *hearing* God speak he forgot the sounds of the words. His ears grew dull and then deaf. Through lack of use he lost the power of *speaking* the old words. His tongue grew thick. It lost its cunning. And so gradually almost all the old meanings were lost.

God has always been eager to get to talking with man again. The silence is hard on Him. He is hungry to be on intimate terms again with his old friend. Of course he had to use a language that man could understand. Jesus is God spelling Himself out so man can understand. He is the A and the Z, and all between, of the Old Eden language of love.

Naturally enough man had a good bit of bother in spelling Jesus out. This Jesus was something quite new. When His life spoke the simple language of Eden again, the human heart with selfishness ingrained said, "That sounds good, but of course He has some selfish scheme behind it all. This purity and simplicity and gentleness can't be genuine." Nobody yet seems to have spelled Him out fully, though they're all trying: All on the spelling bench. That is, all that have heard. Great numbers haven't heard about Him yet. But many, ah! *many* could get enough, yes, *can* get enough to bring His purity into their lives and sweet peace into their hearts.

But there were in His days upon earth some sticklers for the old spelling forms. Not the oldest, mind you. Jesus alone stands for that. This Jesus didn't observe the idioms that had grown up outside of Eden. These people had decided that these old forms were the only ones acceptable. And so they disliked Him from the beginning, and quarrelled with Him. These idioms were dearer to them than life—that is, than *His* life. So having quarrelled, they did *worse*, and then—softly—*worst*. But even in their worst, Jesus was God spelling Himself out in the old simple language of Eden. His best came out in their worst.

Some of the great nouns of the Eden tongue— the *God* tongue—He spelled out big. He spelled out *purity*, the natural life of Eden; and *obedience*, the rhythmic harmony of Eden; and *peace*, the sweet music of Eden; and *power*, the mastery and dominion of Eden; and *love*, the throbbing heart of Eden. It was in biggest, brightest letters that *love* was spelled out. He used the biggest capitals ever known, and traced each in a deep dripping red, with a new spelling—*S-A-C-R-I-F-I-C-E.*

Your friend and His,

S.D. GORDON

Questions for consideration:

1. Have you ever heard a "word from the Lord"
   spoken directly to you?

2. When you consider Jesus watching over you,
   how do you picture His face?

LETTER 10

He Who Emptied Himself

George Griffin

Let Christ himself be your example as to what your attitude should be. For he, who had always been God by nature, did not cling to his prerogatives as God's equal, but stripped himself of all privilege by consenting to be a slave by nature and being born as mortal man. And, having become man, he humbled himself by living a life of utter obedience, even to the extent of dying, and the death he died was the death of a common criminal. That is why God has now lifted him so high, and has given him the name beyond all names, so that at the name of Jesus "every knee shall bow", whether in Heaven or earth or under the earth. And that is why, in the end, "every tongue shall confess" that Jesus Christ is the Lord, to the glory of God the Father.

(Philippians 2:5-11, Phillips)

Dear Questioner,

God is not mere Intellect. He has a heart as well as understanding; he has volitions, desires, sympathies, emotions. "God is love." To sinful passions his bosom is, indeed, inaccessible; but it overflows to infinitude with all those holy sensibilities which he breathed into innocent man with the breath of life. How can reason contemplate such a Being, and yet, without scriptural authority, deny to him the capacity of suffering, even from his own free and almighty choice? Perhaps it might be laid down as a self-evident truism, that the capacity to suffer necessarily results from the capacity to enjoy. The ability of a person of the Trinity to become the voluntary recipient of short-lived suffering may, for aught that speculative pride can urge to the contrary, have been, in the history of eternity, an element not less conducive than his omnipotence, to the prosperity of the universe and the glory of the Godhead.

On the abstract question of the capacity of the divine nature to suffer of its own free volition, we would not, for ourselves, have ventured gratuitously to speculate. Upon a theme so lofty and so holy, we should have chosen to preserve a profound and reverent silence. But when we find it, as we suppose, recorded in the Sacred Oracles, that the second person of the Godhead actually suffered for the redemption of our fallen race; when our credence to that august truth is interdicted by the hypothesis, "God is incapable of suffering or pain," with a voice of power heard, and echoed, and reverberated along the track of ages; when that hypothesis, to retain its own claim to infallibility, must change into figures of speech some of the plainest declarations of Holy Writ, it becomes the right and the duty even of a private Christian to explore respectfully, yet fearlessly, the foundations of a dogma deeply fortified, it is true, in human authority, and hallowed by the lapse of hoary-headed Time, yet scarcely claiming to repose itself on the basis of Revelation.

That the Son of God should have suffered in his divine nature for the redemption of man is not more startling to human reason than the stupendous fact of his incarnation. If, at the time of the first manifestation of divinity in the flesh, the angel of the Lord, instead of announcing the event to the humble shepherds of Bethlehem, had appeared in the midst of an assemblage of Athenian philosophers, made up from the schools of Zeno, Aristotle, and Epicurus, proclaiming to them the "good tidings of great joy," and benignly expounding the spirituality, the ethereal nature, and all the infinite attributes of him who had formed the worlds and was now cradled in a manger, the incarnation of such a being for the remission of mortal sins must have seemed "unto the Greeks foolishness." The heavenly envoy would have been held "to be a setter forth of strange gods" (Acts, 17. 18). Philosophic incredulity would have treated as a fable of mythology the mysterious message of grace. Peripatetic subtilty might boldly have sought to scan the spiritual anatomy of the revealed God, and dared to pronounce its vain decree, that the holy enigma of his incarnation was a physical or moral impossibility. Yet, if there is demonstration on earth, or truth in heaven, the Son of God, the second person of the glorious Trinity, did, in very fact, become incarnate for the redemption of man....

The illustrious personage who had "emptied himself" was he "who, being in the form of God, thought it not robbery to be equal with God." He was, beyond peradventure, the second person of the Trinity. Of what had he "emptied himself?" He had "emptied himself" of the "form of God" for the "form of a servant." He had "emptied himself" of his celestial mansion to become a houseless wanderer upon the earth. He had "emptied himself" of the ministration of angels to wash the feet of his betraying and deserting disciples. He had "emptied himself" of the glory which he had with the Father before the world was created. He had "emptied himself" of his beatific communion with his august companions of the Trinity.

And, remember, all this He did *for you*.

Your friend and His,

George Griffin

GEORGE GRIFFIN

Questions for consideration:

1. When was the most difficult period of suffering you've ever endured?

2. During that time, how would you describe where Jesus was? What was He doing?

The Eternal, Ever-Speaking Word

William Law

Now if Christ does live within you his presence means that your sinful nature is dead, but your spirit becomes alive because of the righteousness he brings with him. I said that our nature is "dead" in the presence of Christ, and so it is, because of its sin. Nevertheless once the Spirit of him who raised Jesus from the dead lives within you he will, by that same Spirit, bring to your whole being new strength and vitality. ... All who follow the leading of God's Spirit are God's own sons. Nor are you meant to relapse into the old slavish attitude of fear—you have been adopted into the very family circle of God and you can say with a full heart, "Father, my Father." The Spirit himself endorses our inward conviction that we really are the children of God. Think what that means. If we are his children we share his treasures, and all that Christ claims as his will belong to all of us as well! Yes, if we share in his suffering we shall certainly share in his glory.

(Romans 8:10,11 & 14-17, Phillips)

Dear Searching Soul,

Why was the Son of God made man? It was because man was to be made again a divine creature. Why did man want such a savior? It was because he was become earthly, mortal, gross flesh and blood. Now take Christ in this light, and consider man in this state, and then all that is said in the gospel stands in the fullest light.

Thus, "Come unto me, all ye that are weary and heavy laden, and I will refresh you." How poor, how mean, and uncertain a sense is there in this, till you know, that man has lost his divine nature, and is fallen into a world that is all labor, burden, and misery! But as soon as this is known, then how easy, how plain, is the full and highest sense of these words, "Come unto me, all that labor, are weary and heavy laden, and I will refresh you!" I will bring to life that first happy state which you have lost. This is the note, the paraphrase, the expositor, the key to the true sense of every doctrine of Christ; which, though variously expressed to awaken the heart, is only one and the same thing. Thus, "Blessed are they that mourn, for they shall be comforted." But why so? Because he that is troubled at the corruption, vanity, and impurity of his fallen earthly state, has the comfort of the heavenly life ready for him. Again, "Blessed are they that hunger and thirst after righteousness, for they shall be filled." How plain and great is the sense here, as soon as we know, that Christ is our righteousness; and that the righteous life of Christ in the soul, is that life which our first father lost! Therefore, to hunger and thirst after this righteousness, is the one way to be filled with that divine life, that we had lost. Again, "If any man thirst, let him come unto me and drink. And out of his belly shall flow rivers of living water."...

For the Word of God which saveth and redeemeth, which giveth life and light to the soul, is not the word printed on paper, but is that eternal, ever-speaking Word, which is the Son of God, who in the beginning was with God, and was the God by whom all things were made. This is the universal teacher and enlightener of all that are in heaven, and on earth, who from the beginning to the end of time, without respect of persons, stands at the door of every heart of man, speaking into it not human words, but divine goodness; calling and knocking, not with outward sounds, but by the inward stirring of an awakened divine life. And therefore, as sure as that is true, which St. John saith, that this eternal Word "is the light of men, and the light that lighteth every man that cometh into the world," so sure is it, that our savior and salvation, our teacher and enlightener, from whom we have every good thought, is Christ within us....

Your friend and His,

William Law

WILLIAM LAW

Questions for consideration:

1. What do you think you've gained in Christ
    becoming man? In other words, what is your
    personal theology of the incarnation?

2. Do you believe that He might still speak to you,
    personally, today?

LETTER 12

The Pattern toward the Image

Hannah Whitall Smith

Therefore, having such a hope, we use great boldness in our speech, and we are not like Moses, who used to put a veil over his face so that the sons of Israel would not stare at the end of what was fading away. But their minds were hardened; for until this very day at the reading of the old covenant the same veil remains unlifted, because it is removed in Christ. But to this day whenever Moses is read, a veil lies over their hearts; but whenever someone turns to the Lord, the veil is taken away. Now the Lord is the Spirit, and where the Spirit of the Lord is, there is freedom. But we all, with unveiled faces, looking as in a mirror at the glory of the Lord, are being transformed into the same image from glory to glory, just as from the Lord, the Spirit.

(2 Corinthians 3:12-18, NASB)

Dear Spiritual One,

God's ultimate purpose in our creation was that we should finally be "conformed to the image of Christ." Christ was to be the firstborn among many brethren, and His brethren were to be like Him. All the discipline and training of our lives is with this end in view; and God has implanted in every human heart a longing, however unformed and unexpressed, after the best and highest it knows.

Christ is the pattern of what each one of us is to be when finished. We are "predestinated" to be conformed to His image, in order that He might be the firstborn among many brethren. We are to be "partakers of the divine nature" with Christ; we are to be filled with the spirit of Christ; we are to share His resurrection life, and to walk as He walked. We are to be one with Him, as He is one with the Father; and the glory God gave to Him, He is to give to us. And when all this is brought to pass, then, and not until then, will God's purpose in our creation be fully accomplished, and we stand forth "in his image and after his likeness."

Our likeness to His image is an accomplished fact in the mind of God, but we are, so to speak, in the factory as yet, and the great master Workman is at work upon us. "It doth not yet appear what we shall be: but we know that, when he shall appear, we shall be like him; for we shall see him as he is."

And so it is written: "The first man Adam was made a living soul; the last Adam was made a quickening spirit. Howbeit that was not first which is spiritual, but that which is natural; and afterward that which is spiritual. The first man is of the earth, earthy; the second man is the Lord from heaven. As is the earthly, such are they also that are earthy; and as is the heavenly, such are they also that are heavenly. And as we have borne the image of the earthly, we shall also bear the image of the heavenly."

It is deeply interesting to see that this process, which was begun in Genesis, is declared to be completed in Revelation, where the "one like unto the Son of man" gave to John this significant message to the overcomers: "Him that overcometh will I make a pillar in the temple of my God; and he shall go no more out: and I will write upon him the name of my God, and the name of the city of my God which is new Jerusalem, which cometh down out of heaven from my God: and I will write upon him my new name." Since *name* always means character in the Bible, this message can only mean that at last God's purpose is accomplished, and the spiritual evolution of man is completed—he has been made, what God intended from the first, so truly into His likeness and image, as to merit having written upon him the name of God!

Words fail before such a glorious destiny as this! But our Lord foreshadows it in His wonderful prayer when He asks for His brethren that "they all may be one; as thou, Father, art in me, and I in thee, that they also may be one in us: that the world may believe that thou hast sent me. And the glory which thou gavest me I have given them: that they may be one even as we are one. I in them, and thou in me, that they may be made perfect in one." Could oneness be closer or more complete?

Paul also foreshadows this glorious consummation when he declares that if we suffer with Christ we shall also be glorified together with Him, and when he asserts that the "sufferings of this present time are not worthy to be compared with the glory that shall be revealed in us." The whole Creation waits for the revealing of this glory, for Paul goes on to say that the "earnest expectation of the creature waiteth for the manifestation of the sons of God." And he adds finally: "And not only they, but ourselves also, which have the first fruits of the Spirit, even we ourselves groan within ourselves, waiting for the adoption, to wit, the redemption of our body."

In view of such a glorious destiny, at which I dare not do more than hint, shall we not cheerfully welcome the processes, however painful they may be, by which we are to reach it? And shall we not strive eagerly and earnestly to be "laborers together with God" in helping to bring it about? He is the great master Builder, but He wants our co-operation in building up the fabric of our characters, and He exhorts us to take heed how we build. We are all of us at every moment of our lives engaged in this building.

Your friend and His,

HANNAH WHITALL SMITH

Questions for consideration:

1. What part of your personal character do you sense Jesus is working on right now?

2. What part of your personal character do you *desire* that He might work on next?

LETTER 13

A Higher Self-Consciousness

Paul Wernle

We dare to say such things because of the confidence we have in God through Christ, and not because we are confident of our own powers. It is God who makes us competent administrators of the new agreement, and we deal not in the letter but in the Spirit. The letter of the Law leads to the death of the soul; the spirit of God alone can give life to the soul.

The administration of the Law which was engraved in stone (and which led in fact to spiritual death) was so magnificent that the Israelites were unable to look unflinchingly at Moses' face, for it was alight with heavenly splendour. Now if the old administration held such heavenly, even though transitory, splendour, can we not see what a much more glorious thing is the new administration of the Spirit of life? If to administer a system which is to end in condemning men was a splendid task, how infinitely more splendid is it to administer a system which ends in making men good! And while it is true that the former temporary glory has been completely eclipsed by the latter, we do well to remember that is eclipsed simply because the present permanent plan is such a very much more glorious thing than the old.

(2 Corinthians 3:4-11, Phillips)

Dear Listener,

This faith arose because a layman, Jesus of Nazareth, endowed with a self-consciousness more than prophetic, came forward and attached men so firmly to His person that, in spite of His shameful death, they were ready both to live for Him and to die for Him. Jesus imparted new values to things: He scattered new thoughts broadcast in the world. But it was only His person that gave these new values and these new thoughts that victorious power which transformed the world....

So what is the starting-point of our enquiry? Not the titles of Jesus; their meaning has itself partly to be explained by the self-consciousness. Not the stories of the Birth, Baptism, and Transfiguration; these are possibly but attempts at explanation on the part of the early Church. No; we must begin with Jesus' testimony to Himself and with His mode of life.

Jesus comes to a man and says to him, "Thy sins be forgiven thee." He does on the Sabbath whatever seems good to Him, and calls Himself Lord of the same. As a new Moses He sets His "But I say unto you" against the words of the law. Himself a layman, He sets Himself in the place of the Scribes and declares to His audience of lay people that all knowledge of

God has been given Him, and that He will impart it to them. He says: "Here is one greater than Jonah, greater than Solomon, the least of whose disciples is greater than John Baptist." He exclaims: "Heaven and earth shall pass away, but My word shall not pass away." He bids all those that labour and are heavy laden come unto Him that He may refresh them. They are to take up His yoke and learn of Him. And, on the other hand, He declares it to be the most grievous sin and one for which there is no forgiveness, if a man should blaspheme against the Holy Ghost who through Him works miracles. He comes to this or that individual with the brief command "Follow Me," and He calls for an immediate break with his previous mode of life. If need be, all are to be able to suffer and to die for Him and for His cause. If any man confesses Him before men and suffers for Him, then Jesus will certainly plead for him in the day of judgment.

These passages have all been taken from the Synoptists; they are the more significant, because Jesus does not here, as in the Fourth Gospel, press His personality upon men's notice, but rather conceals it. Now it is clear that a self-consciousness that is more than merely human speaks from these words. And this is the mystery of the origin of Christianity. What we need to do above all is to accept it as a fact—a fact which demands a patient and reverent hearing....

I ask you: Are your ears open to hear?

Your friend and His,

P. Wernle

PAUL WERNLE

Questions for consideration:

1. Have there ever been seasons for you when Jesus felt like He was playing "hide and seek"?

2. What is your favorite thing that Jesus says about Himself in the four Gospels?

LETTER 14

His Innumerable Titles

Basil the Great

You can now hope for a perfect inheritance beyond the reach of change and decay, "reserved" in Heaven for you. And in the meantime you are guarded by the power of God operating through your faith, till you enter fully into the salvation which is all ready for the denouement of the last day.

This means tremendous joy to you, I know, even though you are temporarily harassed by all kinds of trials and temptations. This is no accident—it happens to prove your faith, which is infinitely more valuable than gold, and gold, as you know, even though it is ultimately perishable, must be purified by fire. This proving of your faith is planned to bring you praise and honour and glory in the day when Jesus Christ reveals himself. And though you have never seen him, yet I know that you love him. At present you trust him without being able to see him, and even now he brings you a joy that words cannot express and which has in it a hint of the glories of Heaven; and all the time you are receiving the result of your faith in him—the salvation of your own souls.

(1 Peter 1:3b-9, Phillips)

Dear Friend of the Son of God,

At one time Scripture uses terms descriptive of His nature, for it recognises the "name which is above every name," the name of Son, and speaks of true Son, and only begotten God, and Power of God, and Wisdom, and Word. Then again, on account of the divers manners wherein grace is given to us, which, because of the riches of His goodness, according to his manifold wisdom, he bestows on them that need, Scripture designates Him by innumerable other titles, calling Him Shepherd, King, Physician, Bridegroom, Way, Door, Fountain, Bread, Axe, and Rock. And these titles do not set forth His nature, but, as I have remarked, the variety of the effectual working which, out of His tender-heartedness to His own creation, according to the peculiar necessity of each, He bestows upon them that need. Them that have fled for refuge to His ruling care, and through patient endurance have mended their wayward ways, He calls "sheep," and confesses Himself to be, to them that hear His voice and refuse to give heed to strange teaching, a "shepherd." For "my sheep," He says, "hear my voice." To them that have now reached a higher stage and stand in need of righteous royalty, He is a King. And in that, through the straight way of His commandments, He leads men to good actions, and again because He safely shuts in all who through faith in Him betake themselves for shelter to the blessing of the higher wisdom, He is a Door.

So He says, "By me if any man enter in, he shall go in and out and shall find pasture." Again, because to the faithful He is a defence strong, unshaken, and harder to break than any bulwark, He is a Rock. Among these titles, it is when He is styled Door, or Way, that the phrase "through Him" is very appropriate and plain. As, however, God and Son, He is glorified with and together with the Father, in that "at, the name of Jesus every knee should bow, of things in heaven, and things in earth, and things under the earth; and that every tongue should confess that Jesus Christ is Lord, to the glory of God the Father." Wherefore we use both terms, expressing by the one His own proper dignity, and by the other His grace to us.

Your friend and His,

ΒΑCΙΛΕΙϚ

BASIL THE GREAT

Questions for consideration:

1. Which of the "titles" of Jesus shared by Basil do you most gravitate to? Why?

2. Is your discipleship with Jesus a present joy—or does it feel more difficult? Why?

Entry into the Timeless Life of God

J.B. Phillips

God has by his own action given us everything that is necessary for living the truly good life, in allowing us to know the one who has called us to him, through his own glorious goodness. It is through him that God's greatest and most precious promises have become available to us men, making it possible for you to escape the inevitable disintegration that lust produces in the world and to share in God's essential nature. ...

We were not following a cleverly written-up story when we told you about the power and coming of our Lord Jesus Christ—we actually saw his majesty with our own eyes. ...

(2 Peter 1:3,4 & 16, Phillips)

Dear Forgiven Heart,

Since most people have not studied the New Testament with their adult minds, and probably have not read it as a whole for many years, they are only too ready to accept someone else's disparagement of the Christian position without going to the trouble of examining the relevant documents for themselves. I think I may claim to know these records pretty well after many years spent in translating them into modern English. And I will say simply that in consequence I have become a hundred times more convinced of their authenticity than when I began the work. After even a moderate familiarity with these brief and sometimes almost naïvely simple documents, it becomes impossible to dissociate Jesus the ethical teacher from Jesus who claimed to reveal the Character of God, who quite naturally forgave sins and who spoke with authority about human life, death and the world beyond death. We may, if you wish, allow that he was sometimes imperfectly reported, and it is certain that we have a very inadequate "coverage" of the most important life the world has ever seen, but the more one studies these brief and incomplete records, the more unthinkable it becomes that they should be mere human fabrications.

For the New Testament as a whole speaks with a new certainty. God is no longer the distant unknowable Mystery; his Nature and Character have been revealed through a man, Jesus Christ. It is now known for certain that God's attitude toward mankind is one of unremitting love. The Master Plan which exists beneath the superficial activities of human beings is now becoming intelligible to them. The reconciliation between the holiness and perfection of God and the selfishness and evil of men has been unforgettably demonstrated. Death, the old dark bogey, has been exposed and resoundingly defeated. And as if this were not enough Good News for human beings to accept, they know now, by the acted parable of the Ascension of Christ, that God and man are eternally inseparable. Humanity is assured of its entry into the timeless life of God. A new dignity has been conferred upon the whole human race for God himself has become a man. New exciting possibilities appear as men begin to understand that the purpose of God's descent to the human level is to enable them to rise and live as sons of God. And what is more, he is prepared to enter human personalities by his own Spirit to make such dreams come true. This temporary life is seen to be no more than the training school for a purpose that points to dimensions beyond the confines of time and space. The center of gravity of the new Faith is not in present earthly activity but in a person and purpose far transcending it.

If Christianity today has degenerated in some quarters into a dull and spiritless moral code, that must not blind us to the tremendous fact upon which all Christian churches are founded. What could be more exciting than to know that the very feet of God have walked this earth of ours, that his authentic voice has spoken to men like ourselves? It is on this issue that we have to make up our minds and adjust our hearts. The Good News may have to be rescued from the encrustations of tradition, the confines of caution, and the dullness of familiarity, but it is still there! The historic fact remains, and we in this now twentieth century, with a conception of God infinitely greater than that of any previous generation, may have to short-circuit the centuries and let the startling truth break over us afresh—that we live on a visited planet.

Your friend and His,

J.B. PHILLIPS

Questions for consideration:

1. On a scale of 0 to 100, how certain do you feel
   of Jesus? (Not "Christianity"—Jesus Himself!)
   Why do you answer that way?

2. If there is one common misconception you'd
   like to correct in others' interpretation of Jesus,
   what would it be?

Love Took My Hand

George Herbert

The Lord appeared...saying: "I have loved you with an everlasting love; therefore I have drawn you with loving devotion... .

"The One who scattered Israel will gather them and keep them as a shepherd keeps his flock. For the Lord has ransomed Jacob and redeemed him from the hand that had overpowered him. They will come and shout for joy on the heights of Zion; they will be radiant over the bounty of the Lord—the grain, new wine, and oil, and the young of the flocks and herds. Their life will be like a well-watered garden, and never again will they languish. ...

"But this is the covenant I will make with the house of Israel after those days, declares the Lord. I will put My law in their minds and inscribe it on their hearts. And I will be their God, and they will be My people. No longer will each man teach his neighbor or his brother, saying, 'Know the Lord,' because they will all know Me, from the least of them to the greatest, declares the Lord. For I will forgive their iniquities and will remember their sins no more."

(Jeremiah 31:3, 10b-12, 33,34, BSB)

Dearly Beloved,

May I share a few verses with thee?

> Love bade me welcome. Yet my soul drew back
>> Guilty of dust and sin.
> But quick-eyed Love, observing me grow slack
>> From my first entrance in,
> Drew nearer to me, sweetly questioning,
>> If I lacked any thing.

> A guest, I answered, worthy to be here:
>> Love said, You shall be he.
> I the unkind, ungrateful? Ah my dear,
>> I cannot look on thee.
> Love took my hand, and smiling did reply,
>> Who made the eyes but I?

> Truth Lord, but I have marred them:
> let my shame
>> Go where it doth deserve.
> And know you not, says Love,
> who bore the blame?
>> My dear, then I will serve.
> You must sit down, says Love,

and taste my meat:
　　So I did sit and eat.

Your friend and His,

Geor. Herbert.

GEORGE HERBERT

Questions for consideration:

1. If Jesus were to write you a "love note," how would it read? Go ahead—write it!

2. How would receiving a note like that inform the way you'd follow Him today?

LETTER 17

Jesus Thinks of Me

Andrew Murray

But you, Israel, my servant, Jacob, whom I have chosen, the offspring of Abraham, my friend; you whom I took from the ends of the earth, and called from its farthest corners, saying to you, "You are my servant, I have chosen you and not cast you off"; fear not, for I am with you; be not dismayed, for I am your God; I will strengthen you, I will help you, I will uphold you with my righteous right hand. ... For I, the Lord your God, hold your right hand; it is I who say to you, "Fear not, I am the one who helps you."

(Isaiah 41:8-10, 13, ESV)

Dear Changed One,

The presence of the Lord Jesus!

That is the secret of the Christian's strength and joy. You know that when He was upon earth, He was present in bodily form with his disciples. They walked about together all day, and at night they went into the same house, and sometimes slept together and ate and drank together. They were continually together. It was the presence of Jesus that was the training school of His disciples. They were bound to Him by that wonderful experience of love during three long years, and in that experience they learned to know Christ, and Christ instructed and corrected them, and prepared them for what they were afterward to receive. And now when He is going away, He says to them: "Lo, behold, I am with you always—all the days—even unto the end of the world."

What a promise! And just as really as Christ was with Peter in the boat, just as Christ sat with John at the table, as really can I have Christ with me. And more really, for they had their Christ in the body and He was to them a man, an individual separate from them, but I may have glorified Christ in the power of the throne of God, the omnipotent Christ, the omnipresent Christ.

What a promise! You ask me, How can that be? And my answer is, Because Christ is God, and because Christ after having been made man, went up into the throne and the Life of God. And now that blessed Christ Jesus, with His loving, pierced heart; that blessed Jesus Christ, who lived upon earth; that same Christ glorified into the glory of God, can be in me and *can be with me all the days.*

You say, Is it really possible for a man in business, for a woman in the midst of a large and difficult household, for a poor man full of care; is it possible? Can I always be thinking of Jesus? Thank God, you need not always be thinking of Him. You may be the manager of a bank, and your whole attention may be required to carry out the business that you have to do. But thank God, while I have to think of my business, Jesus will think of me, and He will come in and will take charge of me. That little child, three months old, as it sleeps in its mother's arms, lies helplessly there; it hardly knows its mother, it does not think of her, but the mother thinks of the child. And this is the blessed mystery of love, that Jesus the God-man waits to come in to me in the greatness of His love; and as He gets possession of my heart, He embraces me in those divine arms and tells me, "My child, I the Faithful One, I the Mighty One will abide with thee, will watch over thee and keep thee all the days."

Your friend and His,

Andrew Murray

ANDREW MURRAY

Questions for consideration:

1. If you could have one day of walking with Jesus in the course of His 33 earthly years, which of them would it be? Why?

2. Do you think He is as present to you today as He was to the original disciples? Why or why not?

The Re-Creation of the World

Henry Drummond

Now when Jesus heard that John had been arrested he went back to Galilee. He left Nazareth and came to live in Capernaum, a lake-side town in the Zebulun-Naphtali territory. In this way Isaiah's prophecy came true: 'The land of Zebulun and the land of Naphtali, the way of the sea, beyond the Jordan, Galilee of the Gentiles: the people who sat in darkness saw a great light, and upon those who sat in the region and shadow of death, light has dawned.'

From that time Jesus began to preach and to say, "You must change your hearts—for the kingdom of Heaven has arrived."

(Matthew 4:12-17, Phillips)

Dear Kingdom Dweller,

The world in which we live is an unfinished world. It is not wise, it is not happy, it is not pure, it is not good—it is not even sanitary. Humanity is little more than raw material. Almost everything has yet to be done to it. Before the days of Geology people thought the earth was finished. It is by no means finished. The work of Creation is going on. Before the spectroscope, men thought the universe was finished. We know now it is just beginning. And this teeming universe of men in which we live has almost all its finer colour and beauty yet to take. Christ came to complete it. The fires of its passions were not yet cool; their heat had to be transformed into finer energies. The ideals for its future were all to shape, the forces to realize them were not yet born. The poison of its sins had met no antidote, the gloom of its doubt no light, the weight of its sorrow no rest. These the Saviour of the world, the Light of men, would do and be. This, roughly, was His scheme.

Now this was a prodigious task—to recreate the world. How was it to be done? God's way of making worlds is to make them make themselves. When He made the earth He made a rough ball of matter and supplied it with a multitude of tools to mould it into form—the rain-drop to carve it, the glacier to smooth it, the river to nourish it, the flower to adorn it. God works always with agents, and this is our way when we want any great thing done, and this was Christ's way when He undertook the finishing of Humanity. He had a vast intractable mass of matter to deal with, and He required a multitude of tools. Christ's tools were men. Hence His first business in the world was to make a collection of men. In other words He founded a Society....

The name by which this Society was known was *The Kingdom of God*. Christ did not coin this name; it was an old expression, and good men had always hoped and prayed that some such Society would be born in their midst. But it was never either defined or set a-going in earnest until Christ made its realization the passion of His life.

How keenly He felt regarding His task, how enthusiastically He set about it, every page of His life bears witness. All reformers have one or two great words which they use incessantly, and by mere reiteration imbed indelibly in the thought and history of their time. Christ's great word was the Kingdom of God. Of all the words of His that have come down to us this is by far the commonest. One hundred times it occurs in the Gospels. When He preached He had almost always this for a text. His sermons were explanations of the aims of His Society, of the different things it was like, of whom its membership consisted, what they were to do or to be, or not do or not be. And even when He does not actually use the word, it is easy to see that all He said and did had reference to this. Philosophers talk about thinking in categories—the mind living, as it were, in a particular room with its own special furniture, pictures, and viewpoints, these giving a consistent direction and colour to all that is there thought or expressed. It was in the category of the Kingdom that Christ's thought moved. Though one time He said He came to save the lost, or at another time to give men life, or to do His Father's will, these were all included among the objects of His Society....

Nothing truer was ever said of this Kingdom than that "It cometh without observation." Its first discovery, therefore, comes to the Christian with all the force of a revelation. The sense of belonging to such a Society transforms life. It is the difference between being a solitary knight tilting single-handed, and often defeated, at whatever enemy one chances to meet on one's little acre of life, and the *feel* of belonging to a mighty army marching throughout all time to a certain victory. This note of universality given to even the humblest work we do, this sense of comradeship, this link with history, this thought of a definite campaign, this promise of success, is the possession of every obscurest unit in the Kingdom of God.

Indeed, it is yours today.

Your friend and His,

HENRY DRUMMOND

Questions for consideration:

1. Write a description of Jesus' "Kingdom of God" (or "Kingdom of Heaven"). What is it like for those who dwell there?

2. Are there specific "Kingdom tasks" He is asking you to complete in the day ahead of you?

LETTER 19

Strange Conquerors We

Edmund de Pressensé

You come to him, as living stones to the immensely valuable living stone (which men rejected but God chose), to be built up into a spiritual House of God, in which you, like holy priests, can offer those spiritual sacrifices which are acceptable to God by Jesus Christ. There is a passage to this effect in scripture, and it runs like this: "Behold, I lay in Zion a chief cornerstone, elect, precious, and he who believes on him will by no means be put to shame."...

But you are God's "chosen generation", his "royal priesthood", his "holy nation", his "peculiar people"—all the old titles of God's people now belong to you. It is for you now to demonstrate the goodness of him who has called you out of darkness into his amazing light. In the past you were not "a people" at all: now you are the people of God. In the past you had no experience of his mercy, but now it is intimately yours.

(1 Peter 2:4-6, 9,10, Phillips)

Dear Ambassador,

The revelations of the Old and New Testament were always given progressively, because it was the will of God to establish a real harmony between the truths which he communicated and the soul by which they were received. This inward, penetrating, progressive action of the Divine Spirit, reaching its ends without doing any violence to human nature, is far more beautiful than any sudden and irresistible operation. Between the two methods there is all the difference between grace and magic. Every one who admits that the ideal of the new covenant shines forth resplendent in the person of the God-Man, must equally admit that the complete blending of the human with the divine element is the great consummation of the Gospel design. This, which is to be the aim of every age, finds its first perfect realization in the age of the Apostles....

Strange conquerors, we must own, are these Galilean fishermen, without repute, without learning, the poorest of the poor, sent forth in their simplicity into the midst of a state of society in which dazzling splendor is combined with a power hitherto irresistible. Brute force will be let loose upon them, and they have neither might nor right to meet force with force; their weapons are to be of the Spirit only. Reviled and persecuted, they must offer no other resistance than the fortitude of their patience and the vigor of their faith; for let them at all avenge themselves on their adversaries, and they will do themselves irremediable wrong by dishonoring and striking a death-blow to their own principle. They are not suffered for one moment to forget that their strength comes from that higher and invisible world, of which they are the representatives upon earth, and which is at once their fatherland and their goal....

For Jesus Christ came to restore the kingdom of God upon earth. He came not simply to offer salvation to every individual man. It was his design to found a holy community, from which, as from a new humanity reconstituted by him, filled with his Spirit and living by his life, the Gospel should go forth into all the world.

You yourself are a representative of the Kingdom of God today. What a high calling is yours!

Your friend and His,

Edmund de Pressensé

EDMUND DE PRESSENSÉ

Questions for consideration:

1. In one short paragraph, write the "mission statement" for your own personal discipleship with Jesus.

2. Is your day-to-day life conforming to the desires of that statement? How so, or how not?

The Bread and the Bliss

Martin Luther

"The work of God for you," replied Jesus, "is to believe in the one whom he has sent to you."...

"I myself am the bread of life. The man who comes to me will never be hungry and the man who believes in me will never again be thirsty. Yet I have told you that you have seen me and do not believe. Everything that my Father gives me will come to me and I will never refuse anyone who comes to me. For I have come down from Heaven, not to do what I want, but to do the will of him who sent me. The will of him who sent me is that I should not lose anything of what he has given me, but should raise it up when the last day comes. And this is the will of the one who sent me, that everyone who sees the Son and trusts in him should have eternal life, and I will raise him up when the last day comes."

(John 6:29, 35-40, Phillips)

Dear Blissful Child,

When one comes to Christ, that is, to his Gospel, he hears the personal voice of Christ the Lord, which confirms the knowledge God taught him, namely, that God is nothing but a very gracious Saviour, who wants to be gracious and merciful to all who call upon him. Therefore, the Lord adds:

> "Verily verily, I say unto you, He that believeth hath eternal life. I am the bread of life. Your fathers ate the manna in the wilderness, and they died. This is the bread that cometh down out of heaven, that a man may eat thereof, and not die. I am the living bread that came down out of heaven: if any man eat of this bread, he shall live forever: yea and the bread which I will give is my flesh, for the life of the world."

In these words the soul finds a well-prepared table, at which it satisfies all hunger; for it knows for a certainty that he who speaks these words cannot lie. Therefore the soul falls upon the Word, clings to it, trusts in it, and also builds its dwelling-place in the strength of this well-prepared table. This is the feast for which the heavenly Father slayed his oxen and fatlings and invited us all to it. ...

The living bread, of which the Lord here speaks, is Christ himself, of whom we partake. If in our hearts we lay hold of only a morsel of this bread, we shall have forever enough and can never be separated from God. The partaking of this bread is nothing but faith in Christ our Lord, that he is, as Paul says in 1 Corinthians 1:30, "made unto us wisdom from God, and righteousness and sanctification, and redemption." He who eats of this food lives forever. Therefore, the Lord says, immediately following this Gospel lesson, where the Jews strove among themselves about this discourse of his: "Verily, verily, I say unto you, Except ye eat the flesh of the Son of man and drink his blood, ye have not life in yourselves. He that eateth my flesh and drinketh my blood hath eternal life; and I will raise him up at the last day."

The bread from heaven the fathers ate in the wilderness, as Christ says here, was powerless to keep them from dying; but this bread makes immortal. If we believe on Christ, death cannot harm us; yea, it is no longer death. The Lord utters the same truth in another passage when he says to the Jews: "Verily, verily, I say unto you, If a man keep my Word, he shall never see death" (John 8:51). Here he speaks definitely of the Word of faith, and of the Gospel....

Therefore, a Christian life is a life of bliss and joy. Christ's yoke is easy and sweet; the reason it seems to us galling and heavy is that the Father has not yet drawn us, and so we have no pleasure in it, neither does this Gospel lesson minister comfort to us. If we, however, rightly appropriated the words of Christ, they would be of much greater comfort to us. By faith we partake of this bread that has come down from heaven, Christ the Lord, when we believe on him as our Saviour and Redeemer.

Your friend and His,

MARTIN LUTHER

Questions for consideration:

1. How would you describe your present hunger for the Lord Jesus?

2. When was the hour or season your life with Jesus was a "bliss and joy"? Remind yourself of the specifics of all that meant and how you were living then.

Name of Jesus!

Gerhard Tersteegen

I was made a minister of that Gospel by the grace he gave me, and by the power with which he equipped me. Yes, to me, less than the least of all Christians, has God given this grace, to enable me to proclaim to the Gentiles the incalculable riches of Christ, and to make plain to all men the meaning of that secret which he who created everything in Christ has kept hidden from the creation until now. The purpose is that all the angelic powers should now see the complex wisdom of God's plan being worked out through the Church, in conformity to that timeless purpose which he centred in Jesus, our Lord. It is in this same Jesus, because we have faith in him, that we dare, even with confidence, to approach God. In view of these tremendous issues, I beg you not to lose heart because I am now suffering for my part in bringing you the Gospel. Indeed, you should be honoured.

When I think of the greatness of this great plan I fall on my knees before God the Father (from whom all fatherhood, earthly or heavenly, derives its name), and I pray that out of the glorious richness of his resources he will enable you to know the strength of the spirit's inner re-inforcement—that Christ may actually live in your hearts by your faith. And I pray that you, firmly fixed in love yourselves, may be able to grasp (with all Christians) how wide and deep and long and high is the love of Christ—and to know for yourselves that love so far beyond our comprehension. May you be filled though all your being with God himself!

(Ephesians 3:7-19, Phillips)

Dear Fellow Poet,

I have been meditating lately upon Luke 1.31: "And behold, you will conceive in your womb and bring forth a Son, and shall call His name Jesus." And now I feel drawn to share these stanzas with you...

> Name of Jesus! highest Name!
> Name that earth and Heaven adore!
> From the heart of God it came,
> Leads me to God's heart once more.

> Name of Jesus! living tide!
> Days of drought for me are past;
> How much more than satisfied,
> Are the thirsty lips at last!

> Name of Jesus! dearest Name!
> Bread of Heaven, and balm of love,
> Oil of gladness, surest claim
> To the treasures stored above.

> Jesus gives forgiveness free,
> Jesus cleanses all my stains,

Jesus gives His life to me,
Jesus always He remains.

Only Jesus! fairest Name!
Life, and rest, and peace and bliss;
Jesus, evermore the same,
He is mine, and I am His.

Oh! is not His life, His presence, so sweet?

Your friend and His,

GERHARD TERSTEEGEN

Questions for consideration:

1. How has Jesus personally satisfied the "thirst" of your heart?

2. What are you "thirsty" to see Him do in your life, even still?

LETTER 22

The Gospel Is Simply Jesus

Origen

Now Christ is the visible expression of the invisible God. He existed before creation began, for it was through him that every thing was made, whether spiritual or material, seen or unseen. Through him, and for him, also, were created power and dominion, ownership and authority. In fact, every single thing was created through, and for him. He is both the first principle and the upholding principle of the whole scheme of creation. And now he is the head of the body which is composed of all Christian people. Life from nothing began through him, and life from the dead began through him, and he is, therefore, justly called the Lord of all. It was in him that the full nature of God chose to live, and through him God planned to reconcile in his own person, as it were, everything on earth and everything in Heaven by virtue of the sacrifice of the cross. ...

I myself have been made a minister of this same Gospel, and though it is true at this moment that I am suffering on behalf of you who have heard the Gospel, yet I am far from sorry about it. Indeed, I am glad, because it gives me a chance to complete in my own sufferings something of the untold pains for which Christ suffers on behalf of his body, the Church. For I am a minister of the Church by divine commission, a commission granted to me for your benefit and for a special purpose: that I might fully declare God's word—that sacred mystery which up to now has been hidden in every age and every genera-tion, but which is now as clear as daylight to those who love God. They are those to whom God has planned to give a vision of the full wonder and splendour of his secret plan for the sons of men. And the secret is simply this: Christ in you! Yes, Christ in you bringing with him the hope of all glorious things to come.

(Colossians 1:15-20, 24-27, Phillips)

Dear Sojourner,

Now the Gospel is a discourse containing a promise of things which naturally, on account of the benefits they bring, rejoice the hearer as soon as the promise is heard and believed. Nor is such a discourse any the less a Gospel that we define it with reference to the position of the hearer. A Gospel is either a word which implies the actual presence to the believer of something that is good, or a word promising the arrival of a good which is expected. Now all these definitions apply to those books which are named Gospels. For each of the Gospels is a collection of announcements which are useful to him who believes them and does not misinterpret them; it brings him a benefit and naturally makes him glad because it tells of the sojourn with men, on account of men, and for their salvation, of the first-born of all creation, Christ Jesus. And again each Gospel tells of the sojourn of the good Father in the Son with those minded to receive Him, as is plain to every believer; and moreover by these books a good is announced which had been formerly expected, as is by no means hard to see.

For John the Baptist spoke in the name almost of the whole people when he sent to Jesus and asked, "Art thou He that should come or do we look for another?" For to the people the Messiah was an expected good, which the prophets had foretold, and they all alike, though under the law and the prophets, fixed their hopes on Him, as the Samaritan woman bears witness when she says: "I know that the Messiah comes, who is called Christ; when He comes He will tell us all things." Simon and Cleopas too, when talking to each other about all that had happened to Jesus Christ Himself, then risen, though they did not know that He had risen from the dead, speak thus, "Dost thou sojourn alone in Jerusalem, and knowest not the things which have taken place there in these days? And when he said what things? they answered, The things concerning Jesus of Nazareth, which was a prophet, mighty in deed and in word before God and all the people, and how the chief priests and our rulers delivered Him up to be sentenced to death and crucified Him. But we hoped that it was He which should redeem Israel." Again, Andrew the brother of Simon Peter found his own brother Simon and said to him, "We have found the Messiah, which is, Christ." And a little further on Philip finds Nathanael and says to him, "We have found Him of whom Moses in the law, and the prophets, wrote, Jesus the son of Joseph, from Nazareth."...

Before the sojourn of Christ, the law and the prophets, since He had not come who interpreted the mysteries they contained, did not convey such a promise as belongs to our definition of the Gospel; but the Saviour, when He sojourned with men and caused the Gospel to appear in bodily form, by the Gospel caused all things to appear as Gospel... For when he had taken away the veil which was present in the law and the prophets, and by His divinity had proved to the sons of men that the Godhead was at work, He opened the way for all those who desired it to be disciples of His wisdom, and to understand what things were true and real in the law of Moses, of which things those of old worshipped the type and the shadow, and what things were real of the things narrated in the histories which "happened to them in the way of type," but these things "were written for our sakes, upon whom the ends of the ages have come."

With whomsoever, then, Christ has sojourned, he worships God neither at Jerusalem nor on the mountain of the Samaritans; he knows that God is a spirit, and worships Him spiritually, in spirit and in truth; no longer by type does he worship the Father and Maker of all. Before that Gospel, therefore, which came into being by the sojourning of Christ, none of the older works was a Gospel. But the Gospel, which is the new covenant, having delivered us from the oldness of the letter, lights up for us, by the light of knowledge, the newness of the spirit, a thing which never grows old, which has its home in the New Testament, but is also present in all the Scriptures. It was fitting, therefore, that that Gospel, which enables us to find the Gospel present, even in the Old Testament, should itself receive, in a special sense, the name of Gospel....

Now what the Gospels say is to be regarded in the light of promises of good things; and we must say that the good things the Apostles announce in this Gospel are simply Jesus. One good thing which they are said to announce is the resurrection; but the resurrection is in a manner Jesus, for Jesus says: "I am the resurrection." Jesus preaches to the poor those things which are laid up for the saints, calling them to the divine promises. And the holy Scriptures bear witness to the Gospel announcements made by the Apostles and to that made by our Saviour. David says of the Apostles, perhaps also of the evangelists: "The Lord shall give the word to those that preach with great power; the King of the powers of the beloved," teaching at the same time that it is not skilfully composed discourse, nor the mode of delivery, nor well practised eloquence that produces conviction, but the communication of divine power. Hence also Paul says: "I will know not the word that is puffed up, but the power; for the kingdom of God is not in word but in power." And in another passage: "And my word and my preaching were not persuasive words of wisdom, but in demonstration of the spirit and of power." To this power Simon and Cleophas bear witness when they say: "Was not our heart burning within us by the way, as he opened to us the Scriptures?"

And the Apostles, since the quantity of the power is great which God supplies to the speakers, had great power, according to the word of David: "The Lord will give the word to the preachers with great power." Isaiah too says: "How beautiful are the feet of them that proclaim good tidings"; he sees how beautiful and how opportune was the announcement of the Apostles who walked in Him who said, "I am the way," and praises the feet of those who walk in the intellectual way of Christ Jesus, and through that door go in to God. They announce good tidings, those whose feet are beautiful, namely, Jesus. ...

If we look at the things by the names of which the Son of God is called, we shall understand how many good things Jesus is, whom those preach whose feet are beautiful. One good thing is life; but Jesus is the life. Another good thing is the light of the world, when it is true light, and the light of men; and all these things the Son of God is said to be. And another good thing which one may conceive to be in addition to life or light is the truth. And a fourth in addition to time is the way which leads to the truth. And all these things our Saviour teaches that

He is, when He says: "I am the way and the truth and the life." Ah, is not that good, to shake off earth and mortality, and to rise again, obtaining this boon from the Lord, since He is the resurrection, as He says: "I am the resurrection." But the door also is a good, through which one enters into the highest blessedness. Now Christ says: "I am the door."

And what need is there to speak of wisdom, which "the Lord created the first principle of His ways, for His works," in whom the father of her rejoiced, delighting in her manifold intellectual beauty, seen by the eyes of the mind alone, and provoking him to love who discerns her divine and heavenly charm? A good indeed is the wisdom of God, proclaimed along with the other good foresaid by those whose feet are beautiful. And the power of God is the eighth good we enumerate, which is Christ. Nor must we omit to mention the Word, who is God after the Father of all. For this also is a good, less than no other.

Happy, then, are those who accept these goods and receive them from those who announce the good tidings of them, those whose feet are beautiful. Indeed even one of the Corinthians to whom Paul declared that he knew nothing but Jesus Christ and Him crucified, should he learn Him who for our sakes became man, and so receive Him, he would become identified with the beginning of the good things we have spoken of; by the man Jesus he would be made a man of God, and by His death he would die to sin. For "Christ, in that He died, died unto sin once." But from His life, since "in that He liveth, He liveth unto God," every one who is conformed to His resurrection receives that living to God. But who will deny that righteousness, essential righteousness, is a good, and essential sanctification, and essential redemption?

And these things those preach who preach Jesus, saying that He is made to be of God righteousness and sanctification and redemption. Hence we shall have writings about Him without number, showing that Jesus is a multitude of goods; for from the things which can scarcely be numbered and which have been written we may make some conjecture of those things which actually exist in Him in whom "it pleased God that the whole fulness of the Godhead should dwell bodily," and which are not contained in writings. Why should I say, "are not contained in writings"? For John speaks of the whole world in this connection, and says: "I suppose that not even the world itself would contain the books which would be written."

Now to say that the Apostles preach the Saviour is to say that they preach these good things. For this is He who received from the good Father that He Himself should be these good things, so that each man receiving from Jesus the thing or things he is capable of receiving may enjoy good things. But the Apostles, whose feet were beautiful, and those imitators of them who sought to preach the good tidings, could not have done so had not Jesus Himself first preached the good tidings to them, as Isaiah says: "I myself that speak am here, as the opportunity on the mountains, as the feet of one preaching tidings of peace, as one preaching good things; for I will make My salvation to be heard, saying, God shall reign over thee, O Zion!" For what are the mountains on which the speaker declares that He Himself is present, but those who are less than none of the highest and the greatest of the earth? And these must be sought by the able ministers of the New Covenant, in order that they may observe the injunction which says: "Go up into a high mountain, thou that preachest good tidings to Zion; thou that preachest good tidings to Jerusalem, lift up thy voice with strength!"

Now is it not wonderful if to those who are to preach good tidings Jesus Himself preaches good tidings of good things, which are no other than Himself; for the Son of God preaches the good tidings of Himself to those who cannot come to know Him through others. And He who goes up into the mountains and preaches good things to them, being Himself instructed by His good Father, who "makes His sun to rise on the evil and on the good, and sends rain on the just and on the unjust," He does not despise those who are poor in soul. To them He preaches good tidings, as He Himself bears witness to us when He takes Isaiah and reads: "The spirit of the Lord is upon me, for the Lord hath anointed me to preach good tidings to the poor, He hath sent me to proclaim liberty to the captives, and sight to the blind. For closing the book He handed it to the minister and sat down. And when the eyes of all were fastened upon Him, He said, *This day is this Scripture fulfilled in your ears.*"

Your friend and His,

ORIGEN

Questions for consideration:

1. Jesus told His followers that He came "not to *abolish* the Law and the Prophets, but to *fulfill* them." What do you think He meant when He said that?

2. Have you ever had the opportunity to proclaim Jesus to someone who didn't know Him? Describe that experience.

Into Liberty from Slavery

Hippolytus of Rome

Praise be to God for giving us through Christ every possible spiritual benefit as citizens of Heaven! For consider what he has done—before the foundation of the world he chose us to become, in Christ, his holy and blameless children living within his constant care. He planned, in his purpose of love, that we should be adopted as his own children through Jesus Christ—that we might learn to praise that glorious generosity of his which has made us welcome in the everlasting love he bears towards the Son.

It is through the Son, at the cost of his own blood, that we are redeemed, freely forgiven through that full and generous grace which has overflowed into our lives and opened our eyes to the truth. For God had allowed us to know the secret of his plan, and it is this: he purposes in his sovereign will that all human history shall be consummated in Christ, that everything that exists in Heaven or earth shall find its perfection and fulfilment in him.

And here is the staggering thing—that in all which will one day belong to him we have been promised a share (since we were long ago destined for this by the one who achieves his purposes by his sovereign will), so that we, as the first to put our confidence in Christ, may bring praise to his glory!

(Ephesians 1:3-12, Phillips)

Dear Free Person,

When he came into the world, He was manifested as God and man. And it is easy to perceive the man in Him, when He hungers and shows exhaustion, and is weary and athirst, and withdraws in fear, and is in prayer and in grief, and sleeps on a boat's pillow, and entreats the removal of the cup of suffering, and sweats in an agony, and is strengthened by an angel, and betrayed by a Judas, and mocked by Caiaphas, and set at nought by Herod, and scourged by Pilate, and derided by the soldiers, and nailed to the tree by the Jews, and with a cry commits His spirit to His Father, and drops His head and gives up the ghost, and has His side pierced with a spear, and is wrapped in linen and laid in a tomb, and is raised by the Father on the third day. And the divine in Him, on the other hand, is equally manifest, when He is worshipped by angels, and seen by shepherds, and waited for by Simeon, and testified of by Anna, and inquired after by wise men, and pointed out by a star, and at a marriage makes wine of water, and chides the sea when tossed by the violence of winds, and walks upon the deep, and makes one see who was blind from birth, and raises Lazarus when dead for four days, and works many wonders, and forgives sins, and grants power to His disciples....

But give me now your best attention, I pray you, for I wish to go back to the fountain of life, and to view the fountain that gushes with healing. The Father of immortality sent the immortal Son and Word into the world, who came to man in order to wash him with water and the Spirit; and He, begetting us again to incorruption of soul and body, breathed into us the breath of life, and endued us with an incorruptible panoply. If, therefore, man has become immortal, he will also be [in] God. And if he is made [part of] God by water and the Holy Spirit after the regeneration of the laver he is found to be also joint-heir with Christ after the resurrection from the dead. Wherefore I preach to this effect: Come, all ye kindreds of the nations, to the immortality of the baptism. I bring good tidings of life to you who tarry in the darkness of ignorance. Come into liberty from slavery, into a kingdom from tyranny, into incorruption from corruption!

Your friend and His,

ἱππόλυτο

HIPPOLYTUS OF ROME

Questions for consideration:

1. What moves you most when you remember that Jesus was *fully God* while yet being a Man?

2. What moves you most when you remember that Jesus was *fully Man* while yet being fully God?

The Extremely Unhistorical Personage

Søren Kierkegaard

Jesus said, "O Father, Lord of Heaven and earth, I thank you for hiding these things from the clever and intelligent and for showing them to mere children. Yes, I thank you, Father, that this was your will."

Then he said: "Everything has been put in my hands by my Father, and nobody knows the Son except the Father. Nor does anyone know the Father except the Son—and the man to whom the Son chooses to reveal him.

"Come to me, all of you who are weary and over-burdened, and I will give you rest! Put on my yoke and learn from me. For I am gentle and humble in heart and you will find rest for your souls. For my yoke is easy and my burden is light."

(Matthew 11:25-30, Phillips)

Dear Invited One,

Come hither all, all ye—with him is rest; and he will raise no difficulties, he does but one thing: he opens his arms. He will not first ask you, you sufferer—as righteous men, alas, are accustomed to, even when willing to help—"Are you not perhaps yourself the cause of your misfortune, have you nothing with which to reproach yourself?"... But he will not ask you thus, will not in such cruel fashion be your benefactor. And if you are yourself conscious of your sin he will not ask about it, will not break still further the bent reed, but raise you up, if you will but join him. He will not point you out by way of contrast, and place you outside of himself, so that your sin will stand out as still more terrible, but he will grant you a hiding place within him; and hidden within him your sins will be hidden. For he is the friend of sinners. Let him but behold a sinner, and he not only stands still, opening his arms and saying "come hither," nay, but he stands—and waits, as did the father of the prodigal son; or he does not merely remain standing and waiting, but goes out to search, as the shepherd went forth to search for the strayed sheep, or as the woman went to search for the lost piece of silver. He goes—nay, he has gone, but an infinitely longer way than any shepherd or any woman, for did he not go the infinitely long way from being God to becoming man, which he did to seek sinners?...

Who spoke these words of invitation?

He that invites. Who is he? Jesus Christ. Which Jesus Christ? He that sits in glory on the right side of his Father? No. From his seat of glory he spoke not a single word. Therefore it is Jesus Christ in his lowliness, and in the condition of lowliness, who spoke these words.

Is then Jesus Christ not the same? Yes, verily, he is today, and was yesterday, and all those years ago, the same who abased himself, assuming the form of a servant—the Jesus Christ who spake these words of invitation. It is also he who hath said that he would return again in glory. In his return in glory he is, again, the same Jesus Christ; but this has not yet come to pass...

It is the lowly Jesus Christ, a humble man, born of a maiden of low degree, whose father is a carpenter. To be sure, his appearance is made under conditions which are bound to attract attention to him. The small nation among whom he appears, God's Chosen People as they call themselves, live in anticipation of a Messiah who is to bring a golden period to land and people. You must grant that one form in which he appears is as different as possible from what most people would have expected. On the other hand, his appearance corresponds more to the ancient prophecies with which the people are thought to have been familiar. Thus he presents himself. A predecessor has called attention to him, and he himself fastens attention very decidedly on himself by signs and wonders which are noised abroad in all the land—and he is the hero of the hour, surrounded by unnumbered multitudes of people wheresoever he fares. The sensation aroused by him is enormous, every one's eyes are fastened on him, every one who can go about, aye even those who can only crawl, must see the wonder—and every one must have some opinion about him, so that the purveyors of readymade opinions are put to it because the demand is so furious and the contradictions so confusing. And yet he, the worker of miracles, ever remains the humble man who literally hath not where to lay his head. ...

Christ, let me say so with the utmost seriousness, is not an actor; neither is he a merely historical personage since, being the paradox, he is an extremely unhistorical personage. But precisely this is the difference between poetry and reality: contemporaneousness. The difference between poetry and history is no doubt this, that history is what has really happened, and poetry, what is possible, the action which is supposed to have taken place, the life which has taken form in the poet's imagination.

But that which really happened (the past) is not necessarily reality, except in a certain sense, *viz.*, in contrast with poetry. There is still lacking in it the criterion of truth (as inwardness) and of all religion, there is still lacking the criterion: the truth FOR YOU. That which is past is not a reality for me, but only my time is. That which you are contemporaneous with, that is reality for you. Thus every person has the choice to be contemporaneous with the age in which he is living and also with one other period, with that of Christ's life here on earth; for Christ's life on earth, or Sacred History, stands by itself, outside of history.

Your friend and His,

SØREN KIERKEGAARD

Questions for consideration:

1. Practically speaking, what does it mean to you that Jesus is "the friend of sinners"? Who would He spend His time with today?

2. Since you are called to live today "contemporaneous with...Christ's life here on earth," how will you do so? Consider ways you might abide afresh with His alive life in the midst of today's schedule.

His Face, Our Fatherland

Thérèse of Lisieux

God, who gave our forefathers many different glimpses of the truth in the words of the prophets, has now, at the end of the present age, given us the truth in the Son. Through the Son God made the whole universe, and to the Son he has ordained that all creation shall ultimately belong. This Son, radiance of the glory of God, flawless expression of the nature of God, himself the upholding principle of all that is, effected in person the reconciliation between God and man and then took his seat at the right hand of the majesty on high. ...

(Hebrews 1:1-3, Phillips)

Dear Lover of Jesus,

A few lines occur to me as I abide in His presence. I share them with you, hoping thereby to encourage your heart in Him:

> Dear Jesus! 'tis Thy Holy Face
> Is here the start that guides my way;
> Thy countenance, so full of grace,
> Is heaven on earth, for me, to-day.
> And love finds holy charms for me
> In Thy sweet eyes with tear-drops wet;
> Through mine own tears I smile at Thee,
> And in thy griefs my pains forget.
>
> How gladly would I live unknown,
> Thus to console Thy aching heart.
> Thy veiled beauty, it is shown
> To those who live from earth apart.
> I long to fly to Thee alone!
>
> Thy face is now my fatherland,—
> The radiant sunshine of my days,—
> My realm of love, my sunlit land,
> Where, all life long, I sing Thy praise;
> It is the lily of the vale,
> Whose mystic perfume, freely given,
> Brings comfort, when I faint and fail,
> And makes me taste the peace of heaven.

Thy face, in its unearthly grace,
Is like the divinest myrrh to me,
That on my heart I gladly place;
It is my lyre of melody;
My rest—my comfort—is Thy Face.

My only wealth, Lord! is Thy Face;
I ask naught else than this from Thee;
Hid in the secret of that Face,
The more I shall resemble Thee!
Oh, leave on me some impress faint
Of Thy sweet, humble, patient Face,
And soon I shall become a saint,
And draw me to Thy saving grace.

So, in the secret of Thy Face,
Oh! hide me, hide me, Jesus blest!
There let me find its hidden grace,
Its holy fires, and, in heaven's rest,
Its rapturous kiss, in Thy embrace!

I ask: How do these words strike you?

Your friend and His,

THÉRÈSE OF LISIEUX

Questions for consideration:

1. What has your "prayer life" been like of late? What have you been most active in praying for?

2. Apart from worship services, how do you find ways to worship Jesus in your daily and weekly life?

Till We Love Him

Daniel Steele

I am deeply grateful to our Lord Jesus Christ (to whom I owe all that I have accomplished) for trusting me enough to appoint me his minister, despite the fact that I had previously blasphemed his name, persecuted his Church and damaged his cause. I believe he was merciful to me because what I did was done in the ignorance of a man without faith, and then he poured out his grace upon me, giving me tremendous faith in, and love for, himself. This statement is completely reliable and should be universally accepted:—"Christ Jesus entered the world to rescue sinners". I realise that I was the worst of them all, and that because of this very fact God was particularly merciful to me. It was a kind of demonstration of the extent of Christ's patience towards the worst of men, to serve as an example to all who in the future should trust him for eternal life.

So to the king of all ages, the immortal, invisible, and only God, be honour and glory for ever and ever!

(1 Timothy 1:12-17, Phillips)

Dear Blameless Friend,

We are exhorted to grow in grace and in the knowledge of Jesus Christ. Some tell us that we find the true philosophy of Christian growth by reversing this order, and putting the knowledge of Christ first, as the means of increasing in grace. But the order of the apostle—grace first and knowledge second—is the most philosophical. We grow in the knowledge of Christ through the heart, and not through the head.

We do not know Jesus till we love him, and the more we love the more intimate our knowledge of him. The more we familiarize ourselves with the perfect character of Jesus, the more we shall admire him, just as by studying the works of Michelangelo we come to admire him the more. But admiration is not love. It kindles no furnace-glow in the affections; it impels the soul onward through no losses and labors, self-denials and persecutions, to the martyr's stake. As the character of Christ folds its splendors beneath the long and earnest gaze of the student, he may be growing esthetically by familiarity with so many moral beauties, and he may become more perfectly grounded in his theological beliefs respecting the Divinity of the man of Nazareth, and yet he may, in his own heart, be refusing to receive and enthrone him as his rightful king. ...

My Brother or Sister in Christ Jesus: permit an older soldier to offer a few words of advice to a new recruit in the army of the Lord. An ancient writer has wisely said, that there have been from the beginning two orders of Christians. The one live a harmless life, doing many good works, abstaining from gross evils, and attending the ordinances of God, but waging no downright earnest warfare against the world, nor making strenuous efforts for the promotion of Christ's kingdom, nor aiming at special spiritual excellence, but at the average attainments of their neighbors. The other class of Christians not only abstain from every form of vice, but they are zealous of every kind of good works. They attend all the ordinances of God. They use all diligence to attain the whole mind that was in Christ, and to walk in the very footsteps of their beloved Master. They unhesitatingly trample on every pleasure which disqualifies for the highest usefulness. They deny themselves, not only of indulgences expressly forbidden, but of those which by experience they have found to diminish their enjoyment of God. They take up their cross daily. At the morning's dawn they cry, "Glorify thyself in me this day, O blessed Jesus!" It is more than their meat and drink to do their heavenly Father's will. They are not Quietists, ever lingering in secret places delighting in the ecstacies of enraptured devotion; they go forth from the closet, as Moses came from the mount of God, with faces radiant with the divine glory; and, visiting the groveling and sensual, they prove by lip and life the divineness of the Gospel. Men tremble before them as Satan in Paradise Lost, when he first saw the sinless pair in Eden, "trembled to behold how awful goodness is."

Next to the power of Jesus, the living Head, these earnest believers preserve and perpetuate the Church from age to age. The secret of their strength is, that they, by the guidance of the Spirit, found the King's highway up the summit of Christian holiness. They strove, they agonized to plant their feet on that sunlit height. They have left the first principles of the doctrine of Christ, and have gone on to perfection. ...

Having chosen the higher path, do not be discouraged by the obstacles in the way of your entering and walking therein. You are not to remove them by your own strength. You have an almighty and complete Saviour, "able to save unto the uttermost all who come unto God by him." With a submissive will and believing soul, "pray that you may know the exceeding greatness of his power to us-ward who believe." Pray, and faint not.

Your friend and His,

DANIEL STEELE

Questions for consideration:

1. What practices have been most helpful for you in growing in your love of Jesus?

2. What does it mean to you that in this present age you are "preserving and perpetuating" the Church? How are you personally involved in declaring Jesus to the next generation?

The Great Promotion

A.W. Tozer

Jesus called his twelve disciples to him and gave them authority to expel evil spirits and heal all kinds of disease and infirmity. The names of the twelve apostles were: First, Simon, called Peter, with his brother Andrew; James, and his brother John, sons of Zebedee; Philip and Bartholomew, Thomas, and Matthew the tax-collector, James, the son of Alphaeus, and Thaddaeus, Simon the Patriot, and Judas Iscariot, who later turned traitor.

These were the twelve whom Jesus sent out, with the instructions: "Don't turn off into any of the heathen roads, and don't go into any Samaritan town. Concentrate on the lost sheep of the house of Israel. As you go proclaim that the kingdom of Heaven has arrived. Heal the sick, raise the dead, cure the lepers, drive out devils—give, as you have received, without any charge whatever.

"Don't take any gold or silver or even coppers to put in your purse; nor a knapsack for the journey, nor even a change of clothes, or sandals or a staff—the workman is worth his keep!...

"Here I am sending you out like sheep with wolves all round you; so be as wise as serpents and yet as harmless as doves. But be on your guard against men. For they will take you to the court and flog you in their synagogues. You will be brought into the presence of governors and kings because of me—to give your witness to them and to the heathen.

"But when they do arrest you, never worry about how you are to speak or what you are to say. You will be told at the time what you are to say. For it will not be really you who are speaking but the Spirit of your Father speaking through you."

(Matthew 10:1-10, 16-20, Phillips)

Dear Disciple,

To be called to follow Christ is a high honor; higher indeed than any honor men can bestow upon each other. Were all the nations of the earth to unite in one great federation and call a man to head that federation, that man would be honored above any other man that ever lived. Yet the humblest man who heeds the call to follow Christ has an honor far above such a man; for the nations of the earth can bestow only such honor as they possess, while the honor of Christ is supreme over all. God has given Him a name that is above every name.

This being true and being known to the heavenly intelligences, the methods we use to persuade men to follow Christ must seem to them extremely illogical if not downright wrong.

Evangelical Christians commonly offer Christ to mankind as a nostrum to cure their ills, a way out of their troubles, a quick and easy means to the achievement of personal ends. They use the right words, but their emphasis is awry. The message is so presented as to leave the hearer with the impression that he is being asked to give up much to gain more. And that is not good, however well intentioned it may be.

What we do is precisely what a good salesman does when he presents the excellence of his product as compared with that of his closest competitor. The customer chooses the better of the two, as who would not? But the weakness of the whole salesmanship technique is apparent: the idea of selfish gain is present in the whole transaction.

Jesus Christ is a Man come to save men. In Him the divine nature is married to our human nature, and wherever human nature exists there is the raw material out of which He makes followers and saints. Our Lord recognizes no classes, high or low, rich or poor, old or young, man or woman: all are human and all are alike to Him. His invitation is to all mankind.

In New Testament times persons from many and varied social levels heard His call and responded: Peter the fisherman; Levi the publican; Luke the physician; Paul the scholar; Mary the demon possessed; Lydia the businesswoman; Paulus the statesman. A few great and many common persons came. They all came and our Lord received them all in the same way and on the same terms.

From any and every profession or occupation men and women may come if they will. The simple rule is that if the occupation is good, continue in it if you so desire; if it is bad, abandon it at once and seek another. If the call includes detachment from all common pursuits to give full time to the work of the gospel, then no profession or occupation, no matter how good or how noble, must keep us from obeying the call.

The activities in which men engage may be divided into two categories: the morally bad and the morally neutral. The activities of the burglar, the gambler, the dictator, the procurer, the dope addict, the gangster and all who prey upon society are bad; nothing can make them better. The call of Christ is away from all such. This is not to be questioned or debated, but accepted without delay and acted upon at once.

But the majority of our human activities are not evil in themselves; they are neutral. The laborer, the statesman, the housewife, the doctor, the teacher, the engineer—such as these engage in activities that are neither good nor bad. Their moral qualities are imparted by the one who engages in them. So the call of Christ is not away from such things, for they may be sanctified by the prayer and faith of the individual, and thus turned into a positive good.

One thing is certain: the call of Christ is always a promotion. Were Christ to call a king from his throne to preach the gospel to some tribe of aborigines, that king would be elevated above anything he had known before. Any movement toward Christ is ascent, and any direction away from Him is down.

Yet though we recognize the honor bestowed upon us, there is no place for pride, for the follower of Christ must shoulder his cross and a cross is an object of shame and a symbol of rejection.

Before God and the angels it is a great honor to follow Christ, but before men it is not so. The Christ the world pretends now to honor was once rejected and crucified by that same world. The great saint is honored only after he is dead. Rarely is he known as a saint while he lives. The plaudits of the world come too late, when he can no longer hear them; and perhaps it is better that way. Not many are self-less enough to endure honor without injury to their souls.

In those early Galilean days Christ's followers heard His call, forsook the old life, attached them-selves to Him, began to obey His teachings and joined themselves to His band of disciples. This total commitment was their confirmation of faith. Nothing less would do.

And it is not different today. He calls us to leave the old life and to begin the new. There must never be any vacuum, never any place of neutrality where the world cannot identify us. Peter warming himself at the world's fire and trying to seem unconcerned is an example of the kind of halfway discipleship too many are satisfied with. The martyr leaping up in the arena, demanding to be thrown to the lions along with his suffering brethren, is an example of the only kind of dedication that God approves.

My friend, let us walk as those ones so approved.

Your friend and His,

A. W. Tozer

A.W. TOZER

Questions for consideration:

1. Take time to write the story of how Jesus first called you. Remember, reflect, be refilled with joy!

2. How have you personally suffered for the sake of following Jesus? How did He uphold you during that time?

In Thy Footsteps, O Jesus!

François Fénelon

Then he spoke to them all. "If anyone wants to follow in my footsteps, he must give up all right to himself, carry his cross every day and keep close behind me. For the man who wants to save his life will lose it, but the man who loses his life for my sake will save it. For what is the use of a man gaining the whole world if he loses or forfeits his own soul? If anyone is ashamed of me and my words, the Son of Man will be ashamed of him, when he comes in his glory and the glory of the Father and the holy angels. I tell you the simple truth—there are men standing here today who will not taste death until they have seen the kingdom of God!"

(Luke 9:23-27, Phillips)

Dear Follower of the Way,

We must imitate Jesus; live as He lived, think as He thought, and be conformed to his image, which is the seal of our sanctification.

What a contrast! Nothingness strives to be something, and the Omnipotent becomes nothing! I will be nothing with Thee, my Lord! I offer Thee the pride and vanity which have possessed me hitherto. Help Thou my will; remove from me occasions of my stumbling; *turn away mine eyes from beholding vanity* (Psalm cxviii. 37); let me behold nothing but Thee and myself in thy presence, that I may understand what I am and what Thou art.

Jesus Christ was born in a stable; he was obliged to fly into Egypt; thirty years of his life were spent in a workshop; he suffered hunger, thirst, and weariness; he was poor, despised and miserable; he taught the doctrines of Heaven, and no one would listen. The great and the wise persecuted and took him, subjected him to frightful torments, treated him as a slave and put him to death between two malefactors, having preferred to give liberty to a robber, rather than to suffer him to escape. Such was the life which our Lord chose; while we are horrified at any kind of humiliation, and cannot bear the slightest appearance of contempt.

Let us compare our lives with that of Jesus Christ, reflecting that he was the Master and that we are the servants; that He was all-powerful, and that we are but weakness; that he was abased and that we are exalted. Let us so constantly bear our wretchedness in mind, that we may have nothing but contempt for ourselves. With what face can we despise others, and dwell upon their faults, when we ourselves are filled with nothing else? Let us begin to walk in the path which our Saviour has marked out, for it is the only one that can lead us to Him.

And how can we expect to find Jesus if we do not seek Him in the states of his earthly life, in loneliness and silence, in poverty and suffering, in persecution and contempt, in annihilation and the cross? The saints find him in heaven, in the splendors of glory and in unspeakable pleasures; but it is only after having dwelt with Him on earth in reproaches, in pain and in humiliation. To be a Christian is to be an imitator of Jesus Christ. In what can we imitate Him if not in his humiliation? Nothing else can bring us near to Him. We may adore him as Omnipotent, fear him as just, love him with all our heart as good and merciful,—but we can only imitate him as humble, submissive, poor and despised.

Let us not imagine that we can do this by our own efforts; everything that is written is opposed to it; but we may rejoice in the presence of God. Jesus has chosen to be made partaker of all our weaknesses; He is a compassionate high-priest who has voluntarily submitted to be tempted in all points like as we are; let us, then, have all our strength in Him who became weak that he might strengthen us; let us enrich ourselves out of his poverty, confidently exclaiming, *I can do all things through Christ which strengtheneth me.* (Philip. iv. 13.)

Let me follow in thy footsteps, O Jesus! I would imitate Thee, but cannot without the aid of thy grace! O humble and lowly Saviour, grant me the knowledge of the true Christian, and that I may willingly despise myself; let me learn the lesson, so incomprehensible to the mind of man, that I must die to myself by an abandonment that shall produce true humility.

Let us earnestly engage in this work, and change this hard heart, so rebellious to the heart of Jesus Christ. Let us make some approaches toward the holy soul of Jesus; let Him animate our souls and destroy all our repugnances. O lovely Jesus! who hast suffered so many injuries and reproaches for my sake, let me esteem and love them for thine, and let me desire to share thy life of humiliation!

Your friend and His,

FRANÇOIS FÉNELON

Questions for consideration:

1. How are you being called to release your judgment of others? *Who* are you being called to cease judging?

2. The most basic meaning of discipleship is imitation. What is Jesus currently calling you to imitate from His own life?

All Is in Christ

Charles Finney

This is my prayer: that God, the God of our Lord Jesus Christ and the all-glorious Father, will give you spiritual wisdom and the insight to know more of him: that you may receive that inner illumination of the spirit which will make you realise how great is the hope to which he is calling you—the magnificence and splendour of the inheritance promised to Christians—and how tremendous is the power available to us who believe in God.

That power is the same divine power which was demonstrated in Christ when he raised him from the dead and gave him the place of supreme honour in Heaven—a place that is infinitely superior to any conceivable command, authority, power or control, and which carries with it a name far beyond any name that could ever be used in this world or the world to come.

(Ephesians 1:17-21, Phillips)

Dear Chosen Child,

Many advance upon the encouragements of the Gospel as if it were only a peradventure, an *experiment*. They take each forward step most carefully, with fear and trembling, as if there were the utmost doubt whether there could be any mercy for them. So with myself. I was on my way to my office, when the question came before my mind—What are you waiting for? You need not get up such an ado. All is done already. You have only to consent to the proposition—give your heart right up to it at once—this is all. Just so it is. All Christians and sinners ought to understand that the whole plan is complete—that the whole of Christ—His character, His work, His atoning death, and His ever-living intercession—belong to each and every man, and need only to be accepted.

There is a full ocean of it. *There* it is. You may just as well take it as not. It is as if you stood on the shore of an ocean of soft, pure water, famishing with thirst; you are welcome to drink, and you need not fear lest you exhaust that ocean, or starve anybody else by drinking yourself. You need not feel that you are not made free to that ocean of waters; you are invited and pressed to drink—yea to *drink abundantly!* This ocean supplies all your need. You do not need to have in yourself the attributes of Jesus Christ, for

His attributes become practically yours for all possible use. As saith the Scripture—He is of God made unto us wisdom, righteousness, sanctification, and redemption. What do you need? Wisdom? Here it is. Righteousness? Here it is. Sanctification? Here you have it. All is in Christ. Can you possibly think of any one thing needful for your moral purity, or your usefulness which is not here in Christ? Nothing. All is provided here. Therefore you need not say, I will go and pray and try, as the hymn,

> "I'll go to Jesus tho' my sin
> Hath like a mountain rose,
> *Perhaps* He will admit my plea;
> *Perhaps* will hear my prayer."

There is no need of any *perhaps*. The doors are always open. ...

You are right in saying that you have cost Him great expense—but the expense has been cheerfully met—the pain has all been endured, and will not need to be endured again, and it will cost none the more if you accept than if you decline; and moreover still, let it be considered Jesus Christ has not acted unwisely; He did not pay too much for the soul's redemption—not a pang more than the interests of God's government demanded and the worth of the soul would justify.

O, when you come to see Him face to face, and tell Him what you think of it—when you are some thousands of years older than you are now, will you not adore that wisdom that manages this scheme, and the infinite love in which it had its birth? O what will you then say of that amazing condescension that brought down Jesus to your rescue! Say, Christian, have you not often poured out your soul before your Saviour in acknowledgment of what you have cost Him, and there seemed to be a kind of lifting up as if the very bottom of your soul were to rise, and you would pour out your whole heart. If anybody had seen you they would have wondered what had happened to you that had so melted your soul in gratitude and love.

Your friend and His,

C. G. Finney.

CHARLES FINNEY

Questions for consideration:

1. Is there anything of Jesus and His Kingdom that you are desperate to possess? Why?

2. If in fact all that is His is already yours, write a prayer of acceptance for the above desire. It is yours already!

Conditions of Glory, Rest and Blessedness

John Owen

Seeing that we have a great High Priest who has entered the inmost Heaven, Jesus the Son of God, let us hold firmly to our faith. For we have no superhuman High Priest to whom our weaknesses are unintelligible—he himself has shared fully in all our experience of temptation, except that he never sinned. Let us therefore approach the throne of grace with fullest confidence, that we may receive mercy for our failures and grace to help in the hour of need.

(Hebrews 4:14-16, Phillips)

Dear Ready Heart,

Jesus is our captain, our leader, our high priest, urim and thummim, our oracle, our ark, on whom the cloud of direction rests and abides for ever. Would you, then, be with God? Take direction from him by Christ in all your undertakings; so do in deed, and not in word or profession only.

I hope I need not stay to give you directions how this duty is to be performed. The "unction" will teach it you, and your "fellowship," I hope, "is with the Father, and with his Son Jesus Christ." Only now take these few words with you:—

(1st.) *Captivate* all your desires to his glory. Set your hearts on nothing, but with this express reserve,—If it is consistent with and expedient unto the glory of Christ and his kingdom. Be not sick of your own violent desires; but lay all your aims and designs at his feet always, becoming as weaned children before him.

(2dly.) Bear before him a *real sense* of your own weakness and folly, both severally and jointly, if not directed by him, that in his pity and compassion he may relieve you.

(3*dly.*) Keep your *hearts* in that integrity, that you may always press and urge him with his own concernment in all your affairs. This is a thing that none but upright hearts can do uprightly.

(4*thly.*) Actually inquire by *faith and prayer*, what is his will and mind;—do it severally and jointly;—do it privately, publicly;—do it every day, and in days set apart for that purpose. He will assuredly be found of you. You know how easy it were to exemplify all these things by testimonies and instances; but time will not permit....

And these are some of the conditions of God's special presence with you. Pleasant conditions! their performance is your glory, your rest, your blessedness;—not your bondage, not your burden. Not one duty doth God on this account require of you, but it is also your reward. O blessed terms of peace and agreement! Blessed be the great Peacemaker! cursed be the breakers of this blessed agreement! Is this all, indeed, that is required, that we may have the special presence of God with us forever? O how inexcusable shall we be if we neglect these terms!— how just will be our ruin! Behold, I have set before you life and death this day; the life or death of these nations. O choose life! seeing it may be had on such easy, such blessed terms; terms wherein, in doing good to others, you will also do good to your own souls; you will give peace to the nation, and have peace and rest in your own souls.

Your friend and His,

John Owen

JOHN OWEN

Questions for consideration:

1. From John Owen's four-part list, what is the *most natural* action for you in your discipleship with Jesus? Why?

2. From John Owen's four-part list, what is the *most difficult* action for you in your discipleship with Jesus? Why?

LETTER 31

Desire for the Sweetness of Christ

Albert the Great

If you really love me, you will keep the commandments I have given you and I shall ask the Father to give you someone else to stand by you, to be with you always. I mean the Spirit of truth, whom the world cannot accept, for it can neither see nor recognise that Spirit. But you recognise him, for he is with you now and will be in your hearts. I am not going to leave you alone in the world—I am coming to you. In a very little while, the world will see me no more but you will see me, because I am really alive and you will be alive too. When that day come, you will realise that I am in my Father, that you are in me, and I am in you.

Every man who knows my commandments and obeys them is the man who really loves me, and every man who really loves me will himself be loved by my Father, and I too will love him and make myself known to him.

(John 14:15-21, Phillips)

Dear Witness,

Remember: God cannot house where there is no love. So if we have love, we have God, for God is love. Furthermore nothing is sharper than love, nothing is more subtle, nothing more penetrating. It will not rest until it has by its very nature penetrated the whole power, the depth and the totality of the loved one. It wants to make itself one with the beloved, and itself, if it were possible, to be what the beloved is too. Thus it cannot bear that anything should stand between itself and the beloved object, which is God, but presses eagerly towards him. As a result it never rests until it has left everything else behind and come to him alone. For the nature of love is of a unifying and transforming power which transforms the lover into what he loves, or alternatively, makes the lover one with the other, and vice versa, in so far as is possible.

This is manifest in the first place with regard to the mental powers, depending on how much the beloved is in the lover, in other words depending on how sweetly and delightfully the beloved is recalled in the mind of the lover, and in direct proportion, that is, with how much the lover strives to grasp all the things that relate to the beloved not just superficially but intimately, and to enter, as it were, into his innermost secrets. It is also manifest with regard to the emotional and affective powers when the beloved is said to be in the lover, in other words when the desire to please the beloved is found in the will and established within by the happy enjoyment of him.

Alternatively, the lover is in the beloved when he is united with him by all his desire and compliance in agreement with the beloved's willing and not willing, and finds his own pleasure and pain in that of the beloved. For love draws the lover out of himself (since love is strong as death), and establishes him in the beloved, causing him to cleave closely to him. For the soul is more where it loves than where it lives, since it is in what it loves in accordance with its very nature, understanding and will, while it is in where it lives only with regard to form, which is even true for animals as well.

There is nothing therefore which draws us away from the exterior senses to within ourselves, and from there to Jesus Christ and things divine, more than the love of Christ and the desire for the sweetness of Christ, for the experience, awareness and enjoyment of the presence of Christ's divinity. For there is nothing but the power of love which can lead the soul from the things of earth to the lofty summit of heaven. Nor can anyone attain the supreme beatitude unless summoned to it by love and yearning. Love after all is the life of the soul, the wedding garment and the soul's perfection, containing all the law and the prophets and our Lord's teaching. That is why Paul says to the Romans, *Love is the fulfilling of the law,* (Romans 13.8) and in the first letter to Timothy, *The end of the commandment is love.* (1 Timothy 1.5)

Your friend and His,

Albertus Magnus

ALBERT THE GREAT

Questions for consideration:

1. How has the love of Jesus transformed you from who you *were* to who you *are*? Describe both those "versions" of you.

2. Is your life most motivated by *externals* or *internals*, by your *exterior* or *interior* life? Why do you answer that way?

Letting Him Have Us

Frances Havergal

In my opinion whatever we may have to go through now is less than nothing compared with the magnificent future God has planned for us. The whole creation is on tiptoe to see the wonderful sight of the sons of God coming into their own. The world of creation cannot as yet see reality, not because it chooses to be blind, but because in God's purpose it has been so limited—yet it has been given hope. And the hope is that in the end the whole of created life will be rescued from the tyranny of change and decay, and have its share in that magnificent liberty which can only belong to the children of God!...

Moreover we know that to those who love God, who are called according to his plan, everything that happens fits into a pattern for good. God, in his foreknowledge, chose them to bear the family likeness of his Son, that he might be the eldest of a family of many brothers. He chose them long ago; when the time came he called them, he made them righteous in his sight, and then lifted them to the splendour of life as his own sons.

(Romans 8:18-21, 28-30, Phillips)

Dear Holy One,

Consecration is not a religiously selfish thing. If it sinks into that, it ceases to be consecration. We want our lives kept, not that we may feel happy, and be saved the distress consequent on wandering, and get the power with God and man, and all the other privileges linked with it. We shall have all this, because the lower is included in the higher; but our true aim, if the love of Christ constraineth us, will be far beyond this. Not for "me" at all but "for Jesus"; not for my safety, but for His glory; not for my comfort, but for His joy; not that I may find rest, but that He may see the travail of His soul, and be satisfied! Yes, for *Him* I want to be kept. Kept for His sake; kept for His use; kept to be His witness; kept for His joy! Kept for Him, that in me He may show forth some tiny sparkle of His light and beauty; kept to do His will and His work in His own way; kept, it may be, to suffer for His sake; kept for Him, that He may do just what seemeth to Him good with me; kept, so that no other lord shall have any more dominion over me, but that Jesus shall have all there is to have;—little enough, indeed, but not divided or diminished by any other claim. Is not this, O you who love the Lord—is not this worth living for, worth asking for, worth trusting for?

This is consecration, and I cannot tell you the blessedness of it. It is not the least use arguing with one who has had but a taste of its blessedness, and saying to him, 'How can these things be?' It is not the least use starting all sorts of difficulties and theoretical suppositions about it with such a one, any more than it was when the religious leaders argued with the man who said, "One thing I know, that whereas I was blind, now I see." The Lord Jesus does take the life that is offered to Him, and He does keep the life for Himself that is entrusted to Him; but until the life is offered we cannot know the taking, and until the life is entrusted we cannot know or understand the keeping. All we can do is to say, "O taste and see!" and bear witness to the reality of Jesus Christ, and set to our seal that we have found Him true to His every word, and that we have proved Him able even to do exceeding abundantly above all we asked or thought. Why should we hesitate to bear this testimony? We have done nothing at all; we have, in all our efforts, only proved to ourselves, and perhaps to others, that we had no power either to give or keep our lives. Why should we not, then, glorify His grace by acknowledging that we have found Him so wonderfully and tenderly gracious and faithful in both taking and keeping as we never supposed or imagined?...

Suppose you make over a piece of ground to another person. You give it up, then and there, entirely to that other; it is no longer in your own possession; you no longer dig and sow, plant and reap, at your discretion or for your own profit. His occupation of it is total; no other has any right to an inch of it; it is his affair thenceforth what crops to arrange for and how to make the most of it. But his practical occupation of it may not appear all at once. There may be waste land which he will take into full cultivation only by degrees, space wasted for want of draining or by over fencing, and odd corners lost for want of enclosing; fields yielding smaller returns than they might because of hedgerows too wide and shady, and trees too many and spreading, and strips of good soil trampled into uselessness for want of defined pathways.

Just so is it with our lives. The transaction of, so to speak, making them over to God is definite and complete. But then begins the practical development of consecration. And here He leads on "softly, according as the children be able to endure." I do not suppose any one sees anything like all that it involves at the outset. We have not a notion what an amount of waste of power there has been in our lives; we never measured out the odd corners and the undrained bits, and it never occurred to us what good fruit might be grown in our straggling hedgerows, nor how the shade of our trees has been keeping the sun from the scanty crops. And so, season by season, we shall be sometimes not a little startled, yet always very glad, as we find that bit by bit the Master shows how much more may be made of our ground, how much more He is able to make of it than we did; and we shall be willing to work under Him and do exactly what He points out, even if it comes to cutting down a shady tree, or clearing out a ditch full of pretty weeds and wild-flowers.

As the seasons pass on, it will seem as if there was always more and more to be done; the very fact that He is constantly showing us something more to be done in it, proving that it is really His ground. Only let Him *have* the ground, no matter how poor or overgrown the soil may be, and then "He will make her wilderness like Eden, and her desert like the garden of the Lord." Yes, even *our* "desert"! And then we shall sing, "My beloved has gone down into *His* garden, to the beds of spices, to feed in the gardens and to gather lilies."

> Made for Thyself, O God!
> Made for Thy love, Thy service, Thy delight;
> Made to show forth Thy wisdom, grace,
>   and might;
> Made for Thy praise, whom veiled
>   archangels laud:

Oh, strange and glorious thought,
   that we may be
A joy to Thee!

Your friend and His,

FRANCES HAVERGAL

Questions for consideration:

1. Having read these words, how would you describe the meaning of "consecration"?

2. Is there any part of yourself that you feel like you're holding back from the Lord? Why?

The Rare Treasure

Thomas à Kempis

The Lord is my chosen portion and my cup; you hold my lot. The lines have fallen for me in pleasant places; indeed, I have a beautiful inheritance. I bless the Lord who gives me counsel; in the night also my heart instructs me. I have set the Lord always before me; because he is at my right hand, I shall not be shaken. Therefore my heart is glad, and my whole being rejoices; my flesh also dwells secure. For you will not abandon my soul to Sheol, or let your holy one see corruption. You make known to me the path of life; in your presence there is fullness of joy; at your right hand are pleasures forevermore.

(Psalm 16:5-11, ESV)

My Dearest,

When Jesus is near, all is well and nothing seems difficult. When He is absent, all is hard. When Jesus does not speak within, all other comfort is empty, but if He says only a word, it brings great consolation.

Did not Mary Magdalene[1] rise at once from her weeping when Martha said to her: "The Master is come, and calleth for thee"? Happy is the hour when Jesus calls one from tears to joy of spirit.

How dry and hard you are without Jesus! How foolish and vain if you desire anything but Him! Is it not a greater loss than losing the whole world? For what, without Jesus, can the world give you? Life without Him is a relentless hell, but living with Him is a sweet paradise. If Jesus be with you, no enemy can harm you.

He who finds Jesus finds a rare treasure, indeed, a good above every good, whereas he who loses Him loses more than the whole world. The man who lives without Jesus is the poorest of the poor, whereas no one is so rich as the man who lives in His grace.

It is a great art to know how to converse with Jesus, and great wisdom to know how to keep Him. Be humble and peaceful, and Jesus will be with you.

---

1   It was Mary, sister of Martha and Lazarus, who so rose, not Mary Magdalene. -Editor

Be devout and calm, and He will remain with you. You may quickly drive Him away and lose **touch with** His grace, if you turn back to the outside world. And, if you drive Him away and lose **touch with** Him, to whom will you go and whom will you then seek as a friend? You cannot live well without a friend, and if Jesus be not your friend above all else, you will be very sad and desolate. Thus, you are acting foolishly if you trust or rejoice in any other. Choose the opposition of the whole world rather than offend Jesus. Of all those who are dear to you, let Him be your special love. Let all things be loved for the sake of Jesus, but Jesus for His own sake.

Jesus Christ must be loved alone with a special love for He alone, of all friends, is good and faithful. For Him and in Him you must love friends and foes alike, and pray to Him that all may know and love Him.

Never desire special praise or love, for that belongs to God alone Who has no equal. Never wish that anyone's affection be centered in you, nor let yourself be taken up with the love of anyone, but let Jesus be in you and in every good man. Be pure and free within, unentangled with any creature.

You must bring to God a clean and open heart if you wish to attend and see how sweet the Lord is. Truly you will never attain this happiness unless His grace prepares you and draws you on so that you may forsake all things to be united with Him alone.

When the grace of God comes to a man he can do all things, but when it leaves him he becomes poor and weak, abandoned, as it were, to affliction. Yet, in this condition he should not become dejected or despair. On the contrary, he should calmly await the will of God and bear whatever befalls him in praise of Jesus Christ, for after winter comes summer, after night, the day, and after the storm, a great calm.

Your friend and His,

Thomæ De Kempis

THOMAS À KEMPIS

Questions for consideration:

1. Go back and revisit your answer to Question 2 from Chapter 1: *How would you describe His proximity now, today?*

2. How would you re-answer the very same question as of this day?

Excellencies Pure and Unmixed

John Flavel

How I long that you may be encouraged, and find out more and more how strong are the bonds of Christian love. How I long for you to grow more certain in your knowledge and more sure in your grasp of God himself. May your spiritual experience become richer as you see more and more fully God's great secret, Christ himself! For it is in him, and in him alone, that men will find all the treasures of wisdom and knowledge. ...

Just as you received Christ Jesus the Lord, so go on living in him—in simple faith. Grow out of him as a plant grows out of the soil it is planted in, becoming more and more sure of the faith as you were taught it, and your lives will overflow with joy and thankfulness. ...

For it is in him that God gives a full and complete expression of himself (within the physical limits that he set himself in Christ). Moreover, your own completeness is only realised in him, who is the authority over all authorities, and the supreme power over all powers.

(Colossians 2:2,3,6,7,9,10, Phillips)

Dear New Creation,

As a theologian long ago said, "There is nothing in him which is not loveable." The excellencies of Jesus Christ are perfectly exclusive of all their opposites; there is nothing of a contrary property or quality found in him to contaminate or devaluate his excellency. And in this respect Christ infinitely transcends the most excellent and loveliest of created things. Whatsoever loveliness is found in them, it is not without a bad aftertaste. The fairest pictures must have their shadows: the rarest and most brilliant gems must have dark backgrounds to set off their beauty; the best creature is but bitter-sweet at best: if there is something pleasing, there is also something sour: if a person has every ability, both innate and acquired, to delight us, yet there is also some natural corruption intermixed with it to put us off. But it is not so in our altogether lovely Christ; his excellencies are pure and unmixed. He is a sea of sweetness without one drop of gall.

"Altogether lovely," i.e. *There is nothing unlovely found in him*, so all that is in him is wholly lovely. As every ray of God is precious, so every thing that is in Christ is precious: Who can weigh Christ in a pair of balances, and tell you what his worth is? "His price is above rubies, and all that thou canst desire is not to be compared with him," Proverbs 8:11.

"Altogether lovely," i.e. *He embraces all things that are lovely*: he seals up the sum of all loveliness. Things that shine as single stars with a particular glory, all meet in Christ as a glorious constellation. Colossians 1:19, "It pleased the Father that in him should all fullness dwell." Cast your eyes among all created beings, survey the universe: you will observe strength in one, beauty in a second, faithfulness in a third, wisdom in a fourth; but you shall find none excelling in them all as Christ does. Bread has one quality, water another, raiment another, medicine another; but none has them all in itself as Christ does. He is bread to the hungry, water to the thirsty, a garment to the naked, healing to the wounded; and whatever a soul can desire is found in him.

"Altogether lovely," i.e. *Nothing is lovely in opposition to him, or in separation from him.* If he truly is altogether lovely, then whatsoever is opposite to him, or separate from him can have no loveliness in it. Take away Christ, and where is the loveliness of any enjoyment? The best creature-comfort apart from Christ is but a broken cistern. It cannot hold one drop of true comfort. It is with the creature—the sweetest and loveliest creature—as with a beautiful image in the mirror: turn away the face and where is the image? Riches, honours, and comfortable relations are sweet when the face of Christ smiles upon us through them; but without him, what empty trifles are they all?

"Altogether lovely," i.e. *Transcending all created excellencies in beauty and loveliness*. If you compare Christ and other things, no matter how lovely, no matter how excellent and desirable, Christ carries away all loveliness from them. "He is (as the apostle says) before all things," Colossians 1:17. Not only before all things in time, nature, and order; but before all things in dignity, glory, and true excellence. In all things he must have the pre-eminence. Let us but compare Christ's excellence with the creature's in a few particulars, and how manifest will the transcendent loveliness of Jesus Christ appear! For,

1. All other loveliness is derived and secondary; but the loveliness of Christ is original and primary. Angels and men, the world and all the desirable things in it, receive what excellence they crave from him. They are streams from the fountain. The farther any thing departs from its fountain and original, the less excellency there is in it.

2. The loveliness and excellency of all other things, is only relative, consisting in its reference to Christ, and subservience to his glory.

But Christ is lovely, considered absolutely in himself. He is desirable for himself; other things are desirable because of him.

3. The beauty and loveliness of all other things are fading and perishing; but the loveliness of Christ is fresh for all eternity. The sweetness of the best created thing is a fading flower; if not before, yet certainly at death it must fade away. Job 4:21, "Doth not their excellency, which is in them, go away?" Yes, yes, whether they are the natural excellencies of the body, acquired endowments of the mind, lovely features, graceful qualities, or anything else we find attractive; all these like pleasant flowers are withered, faded, and destroyed by death. "But Christ is still the same, yesterday, today, and for ever," Hebrews 13:8.

4. The beauty and holiness of creatures are ensnaring and dangerous. A man may make an idol out of them, and indulge himself beyond the bounds of moderation with them, but there is no danger of excess in the love of Christ. The soul is then in the healthiest frame and temper when it is most overwhelmed by love to Christ (see: Song of Songs 5:8).

5. The loveliness of every creature is of a confining and obstructing nature. Our esteem of it diminishes the closer we approach to it, or the longer we enjoy it. Creatures, like pictures, are fairest at a certain distance, but it is not so with Christ; the nearer the soul approaches him, and the longer it lives in the enjoyment of him, still the sweeter and more desirable he becomes.

6. All other loveliness cannot satisfy the soul of man. There is not scope enough in any one created thing, or in all the natural universe of created things for the soul of man to reach out and expand; but the soul still feels itself confined and narrowed within those limits. This comes to pass from the inadequacy and unsuitableness of the creature to the nobler and more excellent soul of man. The soul is like a ship in a narrow river which does not have room to turn. It is always running aground and foundering in the shallows. But Jesus Christ is in every way sufficient to the vast desires of the soul; in him it has sea-room enough. In him the soul may spread all its sails with no fear of touching bottom.

And thus you see what is the importance of this phrase of mine, "Altogether lovely."

Your friend and His,

John Flavel

JOHN FLAVEL

Questions for consideration:

1. As you read this letter, were there any particular sentences or turn of phrases that were especially notable to you? Why?

2. What is the loveliest attribute of Jesus for you as of today? Why do you answer that way?

LETTER 35

Living Oracles of the Church

Joseph Addison

Surrounded then as we are by these serried ranks of witnesses, let us strip off everything that hinders us, as well as the sin which dogs our feet, and let us run the race that we have to run with patience, our eyes fixed on Jesus the source and the goal of our faith. For he himself endured a cross and thought nothing of its shame because of the joy he knew would follow his suffering; and he is now seated at the right hand of God's throne. Think constantly of him enduring all that sinful men could say against him and you will not lose your purpose or your courage.

(Hebrews 12:1-3, Phillips)

Dear Apostle of His,

In the end, we must consider, that many thousands had seen the transactions of our Saviour in Judah; and that many hundred thousands had received an account of them from the mouths of those who were actually eye-witnesses. I shall only mention among these eyewitnesses, the twelve apostles, to whom we must add St. Paul, who had a particular call to this high office, tho' many other disciples and followers of Christ had also their share in the publishing of this wonderful history. We learn from the ancient records of Christianity, that many of the apostles and disciples made it the express business of their lives, travelled into the remotest parts of the world, and in all places gathered multitudes about them, to acquaint them with the history and doctrines of their crucified Master. And indeed, were all Christian records of these proceedings entirely lost, as many have been, the effect plainly evinces the truth of them; for how else, during the apostles' lives could Christianity have spread itself with such an amazing progress through the several nations of the Roman empire? how could it fly like lightning, and carry conviction with it from one end of the earth to the other?...

But to give this consideration more force, we must take notice, that the tradition of the first ages of Christianity had several circumstances peculiar to it, which made it more authentic than any other tradition in any other age of the world. The Christians, who carried their religion thro' so many general and particular persecutions, were incessantly comforting and supporting one another, with the example and history of our Saviour....

St. John, who lived so many years after our Saviour, was appealed to in these emergencies as the living oracle of the church; and as his oral testimony lasted the first century, many have observed, that, by a particular providence of God, several of our Saviour's disciples, and of the early converts of his religion, lived to a very great age, that they might personally convey the truth of the gospel to those times, which were very remote from the first publication of it....

Your friend and His,

JOSEPH ADDISON

Questions for consideration:

1. What is a particular "glimpse" of Jesus that's been entrusted to you to share with others?

2. What does it mean to you that *you* are a "living oracle of the church"? Are there certain places that Jesus is currently calling you to speak of Him?

LETTER 36

Poured Out upon Us

William Penn

Then Peter, with the eleven standing by him, raised his voice and addressed the Pentecost crowds: "Fellow Jews, and all who are living in Jerusalem, listen carefully to what I say while I explain to you what has happened!... This is something which was predicted by the prophet Joel, 'And it shall come to pass in the last days, says God, that I will pour out my Spirit on all flesh; your sons and your daughters shall prophesy, your young men shall see visions, your old men shall dream dreams. And on my menservants and on my maidservants I will pour out my Spirit in those days and they shall prophesy. I will show wonders in heaven above and signs in the earth beneath: blood and fire and vapour of smoke. The sun shall be turned into darkness and the moon into blood, before the coming of the great and notable day of the Lord. And it shall come to pass that whoever calls on the name of the Lord shall be saved.'

"Men of Israel, I beg you to listen to my words. Jesus of Nazareth was a man proved to you by God himself through the works of power, the miracles and the signs which God showed through him here amongst you—as you very well know. This man, who was put into your power by the predetermined plan and foreknowledge of God, you nailed up and murdered, and you used for your purpose men without the Law! But God would not allow the bitter pains of death to touch him. He raised him to life again—and indeed there was nothing by which death could hold such a man. ...

"Christ was not deserted in death and his body was never destroyed. 'Christ is the man Jesus, whom God raised up—a fact of which all of us are eye-witnesses!' He has been raised to the right hand of God; he has received from the Father and poured out upon us the promised Holy Spirit—that is what you now see and hear!"

(Acts 2:14, 16-24, 31b-33, Phillips)

Dear Member of the Body,

The dispensation of the Gospel was the clearest, fullest, and noblest of all other, both with regard to the coming of Christ in the flesh, and being our *one* holy offering to God for sin, through the eternal Spirit; and the breaking forth of his light, the effusion of his Spirit, and appearance of his grace in, and to man, in a more excellent manner, after his ascension. For though it was not another Light, or Spirit, than that which he had given to man in former ages, yet it was another and *greater measure*; and that is the privilege of the gospel above former dispensations. What before shined but dimly, shines since with great glory. 2 Cor. iii. 18: "But we all, with open face beholding as in a glass the glory of the Lord, are changed into the same image from glory to glory, even as by the Spirit of the Lord."

Then it appeared but darkly, but now with open face. Types, figures and shadows *veiled* its appearances and made them look low and faint; but in the gospel time, the veil is rent, and the hidden glory manifest. John i. 5, 17: "And the Light shineth in darkness; and the darkness comprehended it not. For the law was given by Moses, but grace and truth came by Jesus Christ."

It was under the law but as a dew, or small rain, but under the gospel, it may be said to be poured out upon men; according to that gracious and notable promise of God, by the prophet Joel, chap. ii. 28: "And it shall come to pass afterward, that I will pour out my spirit upon all flesh; and your sons and your daughters shall prophesy, your old men shall dream dreams, your young men shall see visions."

Thus we say when it rains plentifully, look how it pours, so God augments his light, grace, and Spirit to these latter days. They shall not have it sparingly, and by small drops, *but fully and freely and overflowing too*. And thus *Peter*, that deep and excellent apostle, applies that promise in *Joel*, on the *day of Pentecost*, as the beginning of the accomplishment of it. This is grace, and favour, and goodness indeed. And therefore well may this brighter illumination, and greater effusion of the Spirit, be called *grace*; for as the coming of the Son excelled that of the servant, so did the manifestation of the light and Spirit of God, since the coming of Christ, excel that of the foregoing dispensations; yet ever sufficient to salvation, to all those that walked in it. This is our *sense of the light, Spirit, and grace of God*: and by what is said, it is evident they are *one and the same principle*, and that he that has light, need not want the Spirit or grace of God, if he will but receive it, in the love of it: for the very principle, that is light to show him, is also spirit to quicken him, and grace to teach, help, and comfort him. It is sufficient in all circumstances of life, to them that diligently mind and obey it....

Wherefore, O my reader! rest not thyself wholly satisfied with what Christ has done for thee in his blessed person outside of thee, but press to know his power and kingdom *within thee*, that the *strong man*, that has too long kept thy house, may be *bound*, and his goods *spoiled*, his works *destroyed*, and sin *ended*, according to 1 John iii. 7: "Little children, let no man deceive you, he that doeth righteousness is righteous, even as He is righteous." *"For which end,"* says that beloved disciple, *"Christ was manifested*, that all things may become new: *new heavens and new earth, in which righteousness dwells."* Thus thou wilt come to glorify God in thy body and in thy spirit, which are his, and live to him and not to thyself. Thy love, joy, worship and obedience; thy life, conversation, and practice; thy study, meditation, and devotion, will be spiritual: for the Father and the Son will make their *abode* with thee, and Christ will manifest himself to thee; for "the *secrets* of the Lord are with them that fear *him:"* and an holy *unction* or *anointing* have all those, which leads them *into all truth*, and they need not the teachings of men. They are better taught, being instructed by the *divine oracle:* no bare *hearsay*, or *traditional Christians*, but fresh and living witnesses: those that have seen with their *own eyes*, and heard with their *own ears*, and have handled with their *own hands*, the word of life, in the divers operations of it to their souls' salvation. In this they meet, in this they preach, and in this they pray and praise. Behold the new covenant fulfilled, the church and worship of Christ, the great *Anointed* of God, and the great *anointing* of God, in his holy high-priesthood, and offices in his church!

Your friend and His,

WILLIAM PENN

Questions for consideration:

1. How would you describe the atmosphere of your "inner life"?

2. What do the words "new covenant" mean to you? What are the differences between the Old and the New?

LETTER 37

To Perceive by Affection

Anselm

For God's word is—'In an acceptable time I have heard you, and in the day of salvation I have helped you'. Now is the "acceptable time", and this very day is the "day of salvation."

As far as we are concerned we do not wish to stand in anyone's way, nor do we wish to bring discredit on the ministry God has given us. Indeed we want to prove ourselves genuine ministers of God whatever we have to go through—patient endurance of troubles or even disasters, being flogged or imprisoned; being mobbed, having to work like slaves, having to go without food or sleep. All this we want to meet with sincerity, with insight and patience; by sheer kindness and the Holy Spirit; with genuine love, speaking the plain truth, and living by the power of God. Our sole defence, our only weapon, is a life of integrity, whether we meet honour or dishonour, praise or blame. Called "impostors" we must be true, called "nobodies" we must be in the public eye. Never far from death, yet here we are alive, always "going through it" yet never "going under". We know sorrow, yet our joy is inextinguishable. We have "nothing to bless ourselves with" yet we bless many others with true riches. We are penniless, and yet in reality we have everything worth having.

(2 Corinthians 6:2-10, Phillips)

Dear Christian Soul,

O Christian soul, soul raised up from a grievous death, soul redeemed and delivered from a miserable slavery by the blood of God, arouse thy mind from sleep, bethink thee of thy resurrection, remember thy redemption and deliverance. Consider where and what is the strength of thy salvation, occupy thyself in meditating thereon, delight thyself in the contemplation thereof; put away thy daintiness, force thyself, give thy mind thereto; taste of the goodness of thy Redeemer, kindle within thyself the love of thy Saviour. With thy mind eat of the honeycomb of His words, with thine understanding suck out their sweetness, for they are sweeter than honey; by loving them and rejoicing therein feed thou upon them, for they are savoury and wholesome withal. Rejoice in that eating, be glad in that sucking out of the sweetness, make merry in that feeding upon them. Where then and what is the power and might of thy salvation? Surely it is Christ that hath raised thee up. He, the good Samaritan, hath healed thee; He, thy good Friend, with His own life hath redeemed and delivered thee; even Christ, I say, and none else. Therefore it is Christ that is the strength of thy salvation....

Behold, O Christian soul, this is the power of thy salvation, this the cause of thy liberty, this the price of thy redemption. Thou wast a captive and in this wise wast thou redeemed. Thou wast a slave, and thus wast made free; an exile and thus brought home; lost and thus found; dead and thus raised up. Upon this, O man, let thy heart feed, this let it inwardly digest, sucking out the sweetness and relishing the goodness thereof, at such times as thy mouth receiveth the flesh and blood of Him, thy Redeemer. Make this thy daily bread and sustenance in this life, and thy provision for the way, for by this and by this alone shalt thou both abide in Christ and Christ in thee, and in the life to come shall He be thy full joy....

Consider, O my soul, consider earnestly, all that is within me, how much my whole being oweth unto Him. Truly, O Lord, because Thou madest me, I owe unto Thy love my whole self; because Thou didst redeem me, I owe Thee my whole self; because Thou makest me such great promises, I owe Thee my whole self, nay more, I owe unto Thy love more than myself, insomuch as Thou art greater than I, for whom Thou didst give Thyself, to whom Thou dost promise Thyself. Make me, I beseech Thee, O Lord, to taste by love that which I taste by knowledge; to perceive by affection what I perceive by understanding. I owe more than my whole self to Thee, but I have no more than this, neither can I of myself render even all this to Thee.

Draw me, O Lord, into Thy love, even this whole self of mine. All that I am is Thine by creation, make it to be all Thine by love. Behold, O Lord, my heart is before Thee; it striveth, but of itself it cannot do what it would; do Thou do that which of itself it cannot do. Bring me into the secret chamber of Thy love. I ask, I seek, I knock. Thou who makest me to ask, make me also to receive; Thou grantest me to seek, grant me also to find; Thou teachest me to knock, do Thou open to my knocking. To whom dost Thou give, if Thou deniest him that asketh? Who is he that findeth, if he that seeketh is disappointed? What dost Thou give to him that prayeth not, if to him that prayeth Thou deniest Thy love? From Thee have I my desire; from Thee may I have also the accomplishment thereof. Cleave thou unto Him, cleave unto Him right earnestly, O my soul! O good Lord, good Lord, cast her not away! She is sick with hunger for Thy love, do Thou cherish her, and let her be satisfied with Thy loving-kindness, enriched by Thy favour, fulfilled by Thy love; yet let Thy love lay hold upon me and possess me wholly, because Thou art with the Father and the Holy Ghost, the one only God, blessed for ever, world without end.

Ah! but my soul grows overwhelmed! More of you, Lord Jesus!

Your friend and His,

Anselmus Cantuariensis

ANSELM

Questions for consideration:

1. Finish the sentence: I OWE JESUS _____.

2. Why were you drawn to that particular answer?

LETTER 38

He Is in the World

John Henry Jowett

The Lord is my light and my salvation; whom shall I fear? The Lord is the stronghold of my life; of whom shall I be afraid? When evildoers assail me to eat up my flesh, my adversaries and foes, it is they who stumble and fall. Though an army encamp against me, my heart shall not fear; though war arise against me, yet I will be confident. One thing have I asked of the Lord, that will I seek after: that I may dwell in the house of the Lord all the days of my life, to gaze upon the beauty of the Lord and to inquire in his temple. For he will hide me in his shelter in the day of trouble; he will conceal me under the cover of his tent; he will lift me high upon a rock. And now my head shall be lifted up above my enemies all around me, and I will offer in his tent sacrifices with shouts of joy; I will sing and make melody to the Lord. Hear, O Lord, when I cry aloud; be gracious to me and answer me! You have said, "Seek my face."

My heart says to you, "Your face, Lord, do I seek." Hide not your face from me. Turn not your servant away in anger, O you who have been my help. Cast me not off; forsake me not, O God of my salvation! For my father and my mother have forsaken me, but the Lord will take me in. Teach me your way, O Lord, and lead me on a level path because of my enemies. Give me not up to the will of my adversaries; for false witnesses have risen against me, and they breathe out violence. I believe that I shall look upon the goodness of the Lord in the land of the living! Wait for the Lord; be strong, and let your heart take courage; wait for the Lord!

(Psalm 27:1-14, ESV)

Dear Heart Made New,

I have been meditating upon Jesus and upon this word written of Him: "He was in the world, and the world was made by Him, and the world knew Him not."—John i. 10.

The past tense sometimes deludes us. The things we look at seem to be so far away. We are spectators of events and not actors. We are critics of the faults of others, and not their fellow culprits. When we read of the doings of far-off yesterdays we so easily assume the voice of the judge on the bench instead of taking our place at the side of the prisoner in the dock. We express ourselves in stern judgment and fiery indignation. We build ornate sepulchres in honour of the prophets whom our fathers murdered. Anybody can wax wroth over the iniquities committed a thousand years ago, but this sort of thing can be combined with a blindness towards similar iniquities in which we share to-day. Therefore it is a good thing to change the tense of the record, to convert it into the present, and to read it as a transcript of what is happening in our time. Let us do so with this great word from the Gospel of John: "He is in the world, and the world is being made by Him, and the world knows Him not." The change in the tense makes the happening immediate. The event is going on. We are actors in the scene. The words beat with the pulse of the present day.

"The world knows Him not!" The unrecognised Christ! He is in our streets. He is busy in our common life. He is making a new world. And we do not know Him! Perhaps He is busy destroying things as a preparative to more constructive work, and we do not detect His presence as these old strongholds of iniquity crumble away. Or perhaps He is working away from the accepted spheres of power and influence and we have not looked for Him in such unlikely places. We have not expected any good thing to come out of Nazareth. We do not anticipate that the great Renewer will be attended by a retinue of fishermen. Perhaps we are looking for something spectacular, and we have no sight for the quieter presences, the less glaring things which enter in at lowly doors. Or perhaps we are giving alien names to things which really belong to Him. We so frequently surrender the Master's treasures to the possession of the world. We fail to see His seal upon them. Some apparently common coin which bears the superscription of the Lord! Some "mere morality" which is really a fruit of the Spirit! Some virtue which is a child of grace! We do not see the marks of the Lord Jesus upon them. In all these ways and in a hundred more our Lord may be in the world, and the world is being made by Him, and we know it not.

Your friend and His,

JOHN HENRY JOWETT

Questions for consideration:

1. What are the parts of your life where you're tempted to relegate Jesus to the past tense? Why?

2. Write the names of those in your life who "know Him not" who you desire would meet Him. Pray over that list.

LETTER 39

Frequenting No Other School

Jean-Pierre de Caussade

"Nobody comes to me unless he is drawn to me by the Father who sent me, and I will raise him up when the last day comes. In the prophets it is written—'And they shall all be taught by God,' and this means that everybody who has heard the Father's voice and learned from him will come to me. Not that anyone has ever seen the Father except the one who comes from God—he has seen the Father. I assure you that the man who trusts in him has eternal life already. I myself am the bread of life. Your forefathers ate manna in the desert, and they died. This is bread that comes down from Heaven, so that a man may eat it and not die. I myself am the living bread which came down from Heaven, and if anyone eats this bread he will live for ever. The bread which I will give is my body and I shall give it for the life of the world. ...

"Unless you do eat the body of the Son of Man and drink his blood, you are not really living at all. The man who eats my flesh and drinks my blood has eternal life and I will raise him up when the last day comes. For my body is real food and my blood is real drink. The man who eats my body and drinks my blood shares my life and I share his. Just as the living Father sent me and I am alive because of the Father, so the man who lives on me will live because of me. This is the bread which came down from Heaven! It is not like the manna which your forefathers used to eat, and died. The man who eats this bread will live for ever."

Jesus said all these things while teaching in the synagogue at Capernaum. Many of his disciples heard him say these things, and commented, "This is hard teaching indeed; who could accept that?"...

As a consequence of this, many of his disciples withdrew and no longer followed him. So Jesus said to the twelve, "And are you too wanting to go away?"

"Lord," answered Simon Peter, "who else should we go to? Your words have the ring of eternal life! And we believe and are convinced that you are the holy one of God."

(John 6:44-51, 53-60, 66-69, Phillips)

Dear Prodigal,

"Jesus Christ yesterday, to-day, and for ever" (Heb. xiii, 8), says the Apostle. From the beginning of the world He was, as God, the first cause of the existence of souls. He has participated as man from the first instant of His incarnation, in this prerogative of His divinity. During the whole course of our life He acts within our souls. The time that will elapse till the end of the world is but as a day; and this day abounds with His action. Jesus Christ has lived and lives still. He began from Himself and will continue in His Saints a life that will never end. O life of Jesus! comprehending and extending beyond all the centuries of time, life effecting new operations of grace at every moment; if no one is capable of understanding all that could be written of the actual life of Jesus, all that He did and said while He was on earth; if the Gospel merely outlines a few of its features; how many Gospels would have to be written to record the history of all the moments of this mystical life of Jesus Christ in which miracles are multiplied to infinity and eternity. If the beginning of His natural life is so hidden yet so fruitful, what can be said of the divine action of that life of which every age of the world is the history?...

I will now become Your disciple, and will frequent no other school than Yours. Like the Prodigal

Son I return hungering for Your bread. I relinquish the ideas which tend only to the satisfaction of mental curiosity; I will no longer run after masters and books but will only make use of them as of other things that present themselves, not for my own satisfaction, but in dependence on the divine action and in obedience to You. For love of You and to discharge my debts I will confine myself to the one essential business, that of the present moment, and thus enable You to act....

Your friend and His,

Jean-Pierre de Caussade

JEAN-PIERRE DE CAUSSADE

Questions for consideration:

1. Why does it matter to your heart that Jesus is presently alive?

2. What are practical steps you can take to more fully "live in the moment" with Him?

It Is He Himself We Have

D.L. Moody

This is my commandment: that you love each other as I have loved you. There is no greater love than this—that a man should lay down his life for his friends. You are my friends if you do what I tell you to do. I shall not call you servants any longer, for a servant does not share his master's confidence. No, I call you friends, now, because I have told you everything that I have heard from the Father.

It is not that you have chosen me; but it is I who have chosen you. I have appointed you to go and bear fruit that will be lasting; so that whatever you ask the Father in my name, he will give it to you.

(John 15:12-16, Phillips)

Dearest Friend,

A rule I have had for years is to treat the Lord Jesus Christ as a personal friend. His is not a creed, a mere empty doctrine, but it is He Himself we have. The moment we have received Christ we should receive Him as a friend.

Your friend and His,

D.L. MOODY

Questions for consideration:

1. Spend some time revisiting your answers throughout the reading of these letters from spiritual guides.

2. How has Jesus moved from being a "creed" or "doctrine" to being your "personal friend" in the midst of these readings and responses? Enjoy remembering—*with Him!*

Notes

ABOUT
SEA HARP PRESS

Sea Harp is a specialty press with one overarching aim: in the words of Andrew Murray, to "be much occupied with Jesus, and believe much in Him, as the True Vine." Our mission is twofold: to reinvigorate the Church's reading of the best of the past, and to bring out fresh editions of both today's and tomorrow's classics — all for the purpose of personal encounter with Jesus Himself.

For every piece of media we consider publishing, we ask two fundamental questions:

- Is this work entirely about the person of Jesus of Nazareth?
- Would the Early Church have thought this work worthy of sharing?

We take our name from the original Hebrew word for the Sea of Galilee—*Kinneret*: כִּנֶּרֶת: meaning "harp"—which was given because of the harp-like shape of the shoreline around which Jesus ministered. It was, in less words, a place known as the Harp-Sea.

Thank you for joining us as we walk the Way with that most wonderful Man of Galilee.

the
SEA *of*
GALILEE

WWW.SEAHARP.COM